C000224507

IMAGES
of Sport

QUEENS PARK RANGERS
FOOTBALL CLUB

Where it all started – St Judes church.

Contents

Acknowledgements

The formulation of this pictorial history has necessarily required two major inputs: photographic material and factual information to enhance the presentation.

I was fortunate to be able to handle the latter need by reference to Mark Shaoul's and Gordon Macey's fine publications relating to the history of the club and I thank them for that and their general assistance.

Selecting the images was more difficult and the endeavours of the club's photographers – John Bough, Ariel Freidlander and John Searight – have proved invaluable. The contributions from Action Images and Associated Sports Photography are also acknowledged.

Other contributions came from Tony Ingham, Tony Chandler, Jim Frayling and the QPR marketing group. My thanks go to all the above and also to James Howarth at Tempus Publishing for assisting me in dealing with some of the problems!

Finally, my wife deserves a mention in despatches for the support given to the project and for also for not talking to me after 7.30 p.m. each evening when I retired to work with my computer!

Tony Williamson

Introduction

In 1942, when I was ten years old, my brother Pat took me to Queens Park Rangers after he had finished his Saturday morning job helping the milkman. For me it was an outing, an event. Little did I realise that I would take that journey on many many occasions over the next fifty years. I still take them now but they are very different. The train from North Wembley to Harlesden, then a number twelve bus alighting on Uxbridge Road is in the past; now it is a battle down the A40 and a search for that elusive parking space.

As a war raged around Europe I was fortunate to be only ten years old; to me the war was an excitement – the searchlights, the shrapnel, the rushing around looking at the bomb devastation, never realising the true significance of what was really happening. For me there was other excitement. What is the next game? Where are QPR playing? Would my Mum let me go? Would my brother take me? The seeds were sown!

In those early years the teams were always changing as the war made its demands on the players, most of who were in the services. Guest players would often make up most of the team, but on such days to me they were Queens Park Rangers. Against that background of the 1940s Harry Brown, Alf Ridyard, Cyril Hatton, Wilf Heathcote, Joe Mallett, Johnny Pattison, Albert Smith and many others were my heroes; there have been many more since! The excitement of promotion in 1948, cup finals at Wembley and QPR reaching the First Division followed.

In 1978, Rangers' finance director Brian Henson introduced me to the club chairman, Jim Gregory, who in 1979 invited me to join the club board. It was an exciting time for the club and for me a tremendous pleasure to be involved. During the eight years I was a board member the club played in cup finals, won the Second Division championship, had seasons of First Division football and European competition.

Along the way I have collected many items relating to the history of Queens Park Rangers and I am pleased to have the opportunity to share some of those with you. I hope you enjoy this brief glimpse into the past, coming as it does at the time when the club have just celebrated 100 years as a professional football club.

I have tried to present this as a pictorial view of the club's history and to reflect its fluctuating fortunes over the years. I have endeavoured to recognise the many people and situations that have contributed to the Queens Park Rangers story.

Queens Park Rangers' star of the twentieth century? Gerry Francis graduated from Rangers' youth scheme and made his first team debut in March 1969. He signed as a professional in June 1969 and was part of the QPR side that were Division Two runners-up in 1973 and Division One runners-up in 1976. In total he made 354 appearances for Rangers, scoring 65 goals. Francis gained his first England cap in 1974 and became England captain in 1975. He played 12 games for his country and netted 3 times. As a manager, he was in charge in the old Division One and the Premier League (when it was created in 1992/93) from 1991/92 to 1993/94 and returned for a second spell in 1998 to maintain QPR's Nationwide Division One status. So far he has been connected with the club for more than thirty years. Other contenders for player of the twentieth century include: the loyal and reliable Tony Ingham, who appeared in 548 games and has had 50 years with the club; Terry Venables, a leader of men who played 206 games and managed between 1980 and 1984, including taking the side to the FA Cup final in 1982 and Division One in 1983); Rodney Marsh, an artist and entrepreneur who played 242 games; and Stan Bowles, who provided quality and entertainment in his 315 appearances.

One

From St Judes to the Football League
1882-1920

1882: Old boys of Droop Street School play as St Judes.

1886: They join with Christchurch Rangers and select the name of Queens Park Rangers. As an amateur team they initially play friendlies. Light and dark blue halves are the team's colours and by the end of the century they have changed their ground eight times.

1892: The club change the team colours to green and white hoops. They win their first major prize, the West London Cup, defeating Fulham 3-2 and go on to win the same competition again in 1893 and 1894.

1895: Win the London Cup.

1898: Turn professional and join the Southern League in the 1899/1900 season. The early years in the Southern League are not outstanding, their best position being fifth in 1904/05.

1907/08: Move to the Park Royal Stadium where the plan was for a 30,000 capacity ground. Win the Southern League Championship and go on to draw with Manchester United 1-1 at Stamford Bridge in the Charity Shield, losing 2-1 in the replay in August 1908.

1912: Win the Southern League for a second time and go on to the Charity Shield at Tottenham Hotspur where they lose to Blackburn Rovers 2-1.

1915-1919: Play during the war seasons in the London Combination League with other London clubs.

1919: Founder member of the Third Division in the Football League – the start of a new era!

The team in this 1897 photograph was under the captaincy of John Musslewhite for the three years up to 1899 when the club turned professional. The skipper had no wish to play as a professional and stood down from the first team when they joined the Southern League and became the regular reserve team captain.

Season 1897/98 saw QPR win their first FA Cup-tie, beating Windsor and Eton 3-0 at home at Kensal Rise. In the next round they were drawn away to Wolverton but the tie was switched to Rangers' ground and in front of a record crowd of around 5,000 they won 2-1. In the second qualifying round they were drawn against Chesham Generals and won 4-0. The main feature of this match was that John Musslewhite was awarded the Sun Medal for the best performance of all players taking part in the third round on that day. Musslewhite also gained representative honours and this photograph shows him wearing his London League shirt and badge. QPR finally went out in the next round of the FA Cup 1-0 to Clapton.

A hurried letter from committee member Arthur Lythaby, around 1897/98, who appears to have a problem in getting the team out for the game against West Ham!

34, BROOKSVILLE AVENUE,
KILBURN,
N.W.

Dear Jack,

May I again ask you to kindly help us by turning out against West Ham on Monday; we are in a hole please turn out & very much oblige

Yours sincerely

Arthur Lythaby

J. Musselwhite Eq

This typical single sheet programme of the era was for a London Cup-tie versus The Casuals in January 1898. The final score was Casuals 1 Rangers 0. Single sheet programmes showing just the team line-ups were the usual style in the late 1890s.

Queen's Park Rangers Football Club.

Balance Sheet. - Season 1888-89.

To Members' Subscriptions	11	11	6	By Rent of Ground	4	10 .
Hon^{ry}		1	12 6	Rent of Dressing Room	5 . .
Rev. Gordon Young		1	1 .	Footballs	3 8 8
John Aird Esqre M.P.			10 6	Subscription to W.L.F.A.	. 10 .
W. Whiteley Esqre			5 .	Stationery Postage &c.	1 8 11
H. Creber Esqre			10 .	Goalposts + Boundary Flags	1 14 1
Sale of Tickets Smoking Concert		4	3 .	Lists of Fixtures	. 17 .
Sale of Fixture Cards		.	11 6	Marking Ground Cup Tie	. 2 6
				Purchase of Towels + washing same	. 9 .
				Smoking Concert Expenses	1 12 6
				Balance in hand	. 12 4
		£ 20	**5 .**		**£ 20 5 .**

The accounts for 1888. The annual turnover was £20 and costs were continuing to rise. Nothing changes: throughout football's history, clubs have gone to shareholders and fans for money from time to time to keep things going and Rangers are no exception.

Certificate No.134

The QUEEN'S PARK RANGERS
Football & Athletic Club, Limited.

INCORPORATED UNDER THE COMPANIES ACTS, 1862 TO 1893.

CAPITAL - - - - - £5,000,
In 10,000 Ordinary Shares of 10s. each.

This is to Certify that _John Musselwhite_ of _264 Kilburn Lane_ is the registered holder of 4 fully-paid Ordinary Shares of 10s. each, numbered 1101 to 1104 inclusive, in "THE QUEEN'S PARK RANGERS FOOTBALL AND ATHLETIC CLUB, LIMITED," subject to the provisions of the Memorandum and Articles of Association of the said Company.

GIVEN under the Common Seal of the said Company the 31st day of _July_ 1899.

Directors.

Secretary.

By 1899 the club have progressed and decide to go professional. This results in a call for capital; 10,000 shares are issued which raise £5,000. Cash injections were to become a regular feature in future years.

12

The Queens Park Rangers team in 1901/02. Left to right, back row: Waters (trainer), McQueen, Jordan, Bowman, Burton, Aston, White, Lennox, Keetch. Middle row: King, Pryce, Millar, Christie, Collins. Front row: Newlands, Seeley, Freeman. After two initial seasons of mid-table performance, this side struggled and finished twelfth with the record of played 30, won 8, drawn 7 and lost 15 with a total of 23 points. They scored 34 goals and conceded 56.

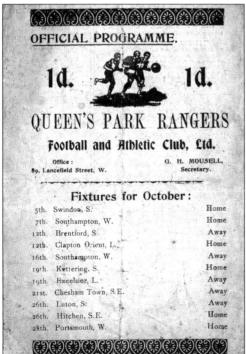

OFFICIAL PROGRAMME.

1d.   1d.

QUEEN'S PARK RANGERS

Football and Athletic Club, Ltd.

Office :   G. H. MOUSELL,
89, Lancefield Street, W.   Secretary.

Fixtures for October:

5th.	Swindon, S.	Home
7th.	Southampton, W.	Home
12th.	Brentford, S.	Away
12th.	Clapton Orient, L.	Home
16th.	Southampton, W.	Away
19th.	Kettering, S.	Home
19th.	Excelsior, L.	Away
21st.	Chesham Town, S.E.	Away
26th.	Luton, S.	Away
26th.	Hitchen, S.E.	Home
28th.	Portsmouth, W.	Home

Queen's Park Rangers.

RIGHT.   LEFT.

Collins

Newlands   Aston

Keech   Freeman   White

Stewart   Pryce   Millar   McQueen   Seeley

Cowan   Davies   Beechn   Bradshaw   Oakley

Richardson   Logan   Codling

Didsdall   Downie

Menham

LEFT.   RIGHT.

Swindon.

REFEREE ... ... Mr. J. T. CLARKE.

F. J. HUNTER,

WINE AND SPIRIT MERCHANT,

'Latimer Arms,'

LATIMER ROAD, NORTH KENSINGTON.

HEAD-QUARTERS OF VISITING CLUBS.

Malt and all kinds of Wines and Spirits of the Best Quality.

The Host will be pleased to give any information required respecting the various Clubs.

An early QPR home programme after the club had gone professional in 1899 and joined the Southern League. This is the team line-up against Swindon on 5 October 1901 when Rangers gained a 4-0 win.

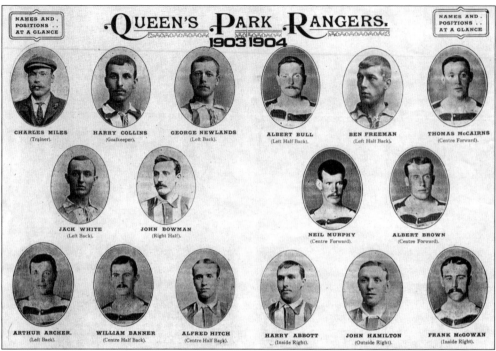

QUEEN'S PARK RANGERS.
1903 1904

CHARLES MILES (Trainer).

HARRY COLLINS (Goalkeeper).

GEORGE NEWLANDS (Left Back).

ALBERT BULL (Left Half Back).

BEN FREEMAN (Left Half Back).

THOMAS McCAIRNS (Centre Forward).

JACK WHITE (Left Back).

JOHN BOWMAN (Right Half).

NEIL MURPHY (Centre Forward).

ALBERT BROWN (Centre Forward).

ARTHUR ARCHER. (Left Back).

WILLIAM BANNER (Centre Half Back).

ALFRED HITCH (Centre Half Back).

HARRY ABBOTT (Inside Right).

JOHN HAMILTON (Outside Right).

FRANK McGOWAN (Inside Right).

The 1903/04 players as presented in the club handbook of that year. The team had their best season to date by finishing fifth in the Southern League with a record of played 34, won 15, drawn 11 and lost 8 with a total of 41 points. They scored 53 goals and conceded 37.

Park Royal, 3 Sept 1904. The QPR forwards take control during a 2-1 win over Plymouth Argyle. Blackwood scored both goals for Rangers in this, the opening game of the season.

William Draper, a relatively young man, was appointed team trainer for the 1906/07 season and he held that position until the war. Only then did he start playing for the club – presumably due to a shortage of players – and he made over 100 appearances between 1914 and 1919. He then returned to his coaching role and was trainer until around 1926.

"Elephant & Castle,"

HARROW ROAD.

Proprietors   ..   ..   ..   MESSRS. NEWBERY & TRATT.

Wines and Spirits ✱ ✱ ✱

✱ ✱ of the Finest Quality.

The Best Bitter in the Neighbourhood.

Fine Billiard Saloon

(Two Tables by BURROUGHS & WATTS).

Marker, WILLIAM KEECH
(Late of the Queen's Park Rangers.)

Results of Matches, Home and Away, will be posted in the Saloon Bar.

QUEEN'S PARK RANGERS' HEADQUARTERS.

William Keetch played for the club from 1899 to 1902, appearing in some 69 competitive matches. He became a 'billiards marker' on his retirement from football and the local billiard hall was quick to use his popularity to bring in the Rangers fans!

The 1904/05 team which finished seventh in the League. Left to right, back row: Miles (trainer), Archer, J. Cross, Howes, Hitch, Downing, Newlands. Front row: Murphy, Milward, Bevan, Ryder, Singleton.

Joy in the County Town.

Brentford knock the Rangers out of the English Cup Competition, at Park Royal, Dec. 10th, 1904.

Ten thousand lovers of the game
  Were there, to view the fight,
When Brentford's band marched hand in hand
  'Gainst Rangers—men of might;
It would have done friend Kipling good
  To have gazed upon the sight.

The pride of " good old Molyneaux "
  Were fit for duty's call;
Shanks, seventeen minutes from the start
  Electrified us all,
Secured a " pass from Warrington,"
  And shot a splendid goal.

With Whitaker in fearless form,
  Watson, and Howarth, grand,
Whilst Parsonage was all the rage
  'Mongst patrons on the stand,
In fact, they cheered to that extent,
  You couldn't hear the band.

Both Oliver and Tomlinson
  Seemed " bright as flowers in May,"
Quite confident of victory,
  And so, methought was Jay,
They seemed to have an aim in view
  Before they hied away.

No, Brentford never flinched one jot,
  Like hearts of oak they stood ;
Swarbrick and Warrington were gems,
  And so was Underwood ;
To have seen Shanks in his element,
  It would have done you good.

Brentfordians missed good Bellingham,
  And Hobson was not there,
Two lads possess'd of nought but grit,
  Willing to do and dare ;
The conquest made friend Lewis feel
  Like " climbing the Golden Stair."

                          A.C.—Cricket Rhymster

During the season Rangers played Brentford at home in the FA Cup and on this occasion the Bees came out on top 2-1. This prompted A.C. (Cricket Rhymster), a noted cricket writer, to pen his poetic review of the match.

16

The Fielding family provided much of the leadership to QPR through the early years of professionalism. They were represented on the board of QPR for over thirty-five years and on a number of occasions kept the club afloat. J.H. Fielding (above left) became chairman in 1907 and in his first season he saw the club win the Southern League Championship. W.L. Wood (above right), the secretary/treasurer, was at his side during all the pre-Third Division days.

James Cowan was manager of the team from 1907 to 1914 and led them to two Southern League championships and into two Charity Shield games. He could justifiably claim to have been Rangers most successful manager through the club's first eighty years.

The team photograph for the 1905/06 season. Left to right, back row: Draper (trainer), White, Yenson, Hitch, Downing, Kingsley, Newlands. Front row: Thompson, Sugden, Bevan, Ryder, Cowan.

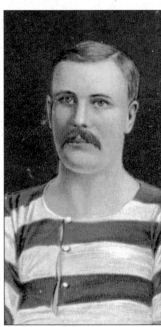

In the early years of this century cigarette cards started to feature a few Southern League players. Yenson (who played from 1905-08), Ryder (1904-07) and Howes (1904-07) were the first three QPR personalities to appear.

E.H.LINTOTT.

Evelyn Henry Lintott of Queens Park Rangers and England. While at QPR, Lintott played 8 times for England, winning 5 amateur and 3 full caps. Signed from Plymouth in September 1907, he only played one full season for the Rangers before his transfer to Bradford City in November 1908. He was chairman of the Players Union for some time before he resigned in 1911. He sadly died on active service during the First World War. It would be sixty-four years before another QPR player (Rodney Marsh) would gain a full England cap!

QUEEN'S PARK RANGERS.

Goal:

RIGHT WING.   LEFT WING.

Shaw

Backs

White   Fidler
2

Half-Backs

Mitchell   E. H. Lintott   Downing
4   5   6

Forwards

Pentland   P. G. Skilton   Walker   Gittins   Barnes
7   8   9   10   11

Referee—Mr. J. H. PEARSON.

TO-DAY'S ☺ TEAMS.

Linesmen—Messrs. S. G. Cassidy and F. J. Caton.

Forwards :

Johnson   Jones   Twigg   Vincent   Hunter
12   13   14   15   16

Half-Backs :

Blythe   Comrie   Frost
17   18   19

Backs

Stevenson   Sutherland
20   21

Goal :

LEFT WING;   RIGHT WING

Joyce
22

MILLWALL.

In event of an alteration in the Teams, a Board will be shown round the Ground.

The 1907/08 team that were to become Southern League Champions. Left to right, back: directors Saltwell, Saxby, Walton, J. Fielding (chairman), Eagle, W. Cross, Hart, Foster, Wood (secretary). Third row: Draper (trainer), Sugden, Downing, Fidler, Webb, Yenson, Ansell, J. Cowan (manager), Waters (assistant trainer). Second row: Shaw, Pentland, Rogers, Walker, Hitchcock, McLean, MacDonald, Barnes. Front row: Mitchell, Gettins, Nichols, Morris.

The programme for Queens Park Rangers versus Millwall on 2 November 1907. This was a special occasion as Rangers opened their new ground at Park Royal, which was planned to be developed to eventually hold 30,000 spectators, Unfortunately, the visitors spoilt the day and Rangers went down 2-3.

The formal opening of the new grandstand on 2 November 1907. The proceedings started with Lord Kinnaird and members of the Football Association arriving by special train and then they took lunch with the directors prior to the game. Following the above photograph session they stayed to see the match against Millwall. The new stadium and the train service saw attendances increase by 27% that season, but perhaps the Southern League championship helped! The season finished with the club having its best average home gates as a Southern League outfit.

The programme for the Charity Shield replay at Stamford Bridge against Manchester United in August 1908. Manchester United made two changes from the first game while QPR replaced Pentland with McNaught. Rangers were well beaten on the day, losing 4-0 in front of a crowd of around 10,000.

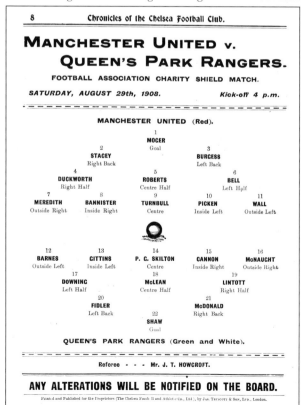

8   Chronicles of the Chelsea Football Club.

MANCHESTER UNITED v. QUEEN'S PARK RANGERS.

FOOTBALL ASSOCIATION CHARITY SHIELD MATCH.

SATURDAY, AUGUST 29th, 1908.   *Kick-off 4 p.m.*

MANCHESTER UNITED (Red).

1
MOGER
Goal

2   3
STACEY   BURCESS
Right Back   Left Back

4   5   6
DUCKWORTH   ROBERTS   BELL
Right Half   Centre Half Left Half

7   8   9   10   11
MEREDITH   BANNISTER TURNBULL   PICKEN   WALL
Outside Right Inside Right Centre Inside Left Outside Left

12   13   14   15   16
BARNES   CITTINS   P. C. SKILTON CANNON   McNAUCHT
Outside Left Inside Left Centre   Inside Right Outside Right

17   18   19
DOWNINC   McLEAN   LINTOTT
Left Half   Centre Half   Right Half

20   21
FIDLER   McDONALD
Left Back   22   Right Back
             SHAW
             Goal

QUEEN'S PARK RANGERS (Green and White).

Referee - - - Mr. J. T. HOWCROFT.

ANY ALTERATIONS WILL BE NOTIFIED ON THE BOARD.

Printed and Published for the Proprietors (The Chelsea Football and Athletic Co., Ltd.), by Jas. Truscott & Son, Ltd., London.

One of the first cigarette companies to feature footballers on cards was Taddy & Co., who issued sets in 1907, 1908/09 and 1913/14, and included fifteen QPR players in each set. This period coincided with the Rangers' best times in the Southern League. The players shown here –

S. Downing, A. Gittins, W. Barnes, J. Fidler, J. McLean, C. Shaw, J. Macdonald and A. Walker
– featured in the 1907/08 League winning side and played in the Charity Shield match in April
1908 and the replay in August.

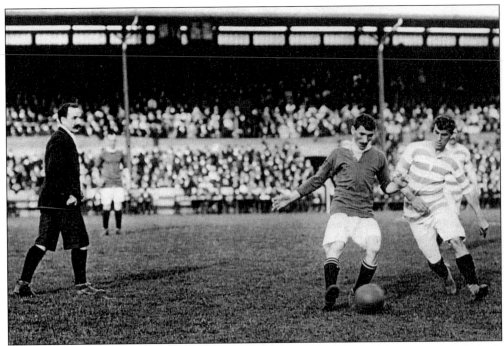

Manchester United's legendary Welshman Billy Meredith shields the ball from Wally Barnes in the Charity Shield match. Referee Howcroft is up with the play.

After the glory of the 1907/08 season, Rangers finished a disappointing fifteenth in 1908/09. The team that lined up for 1909/10 was somewhat changed from the championship team, as illustrated in this pre-season photograph. They gave a good account of themselves, rising to third in the Southern League that season. Left to right, back row: J. Cowan (manager), Goodfellow, Macnaught, Nicholls, Handford, Ashman, Macdonald, Hartwell, Wake, Draper (trainer). Middle row: Whyman, Wentworth, Barnes (captain), Morris, Green, Shaw, Travers, Fidler, Mitchell, Logan. Front row: Bean, Randage, Steer, Swan. The record for that season was played 42, won 19, drawn 13 and lost 10 with a total of 51 points. The team scored 56 goals and conceded 47.

In 1911/12, James Cowan achieved another Southern League championship with this QPR team. Left to right, back row: Saltwell, Fielding, Hart (directors), Wood (secretary). Middle row: Cowan (manager), Butterworth, Wake, McDonald, Shaw, Fidler, Mitchell, Draper (trainer). Front row: Smith, Revel, McKie, Thorton, Barnes. Their record was played 38, won 21, drawn 11 and lost 6 with a total of 53 points. They scored 59 goals and conceded 35.

Archie Mitchell (left) was a great signing from Aston Villa in 1907. He played in both Rangers championship sides and gained Southern League representative honours, including captaining the League against the Football League in 1913/14. A large part of his football career was lost to the First World War, but he was an important member of the Rangers side that made its Football League debut in 1920/21. In later years he rejoined QPR, initially as a member of the coaching staff, but ultimately becoming manager in 1931. In 1912 the club signed a left-sided player from Willenhall Swifts who played some eleven years for Rangers. John Gregory (right) was confident with the ball and also a good passer. His total appearances, like many of his team colleagues, were restricted due to the First World War but he still played 241 matches for the club between 1912 and 1923, scoring 59 goals.

In their second appearance in the Charity Shield, Rangers played against Blackburn Rovers on 4 May 1912 at Tottenham. On a filthy day some 7,000 spectators watched a wretched game which Rangers lost 2-1. Revill scored the QPR goal. The money raised on this occasion was £262 and went to the Titanic Disaster Fund.

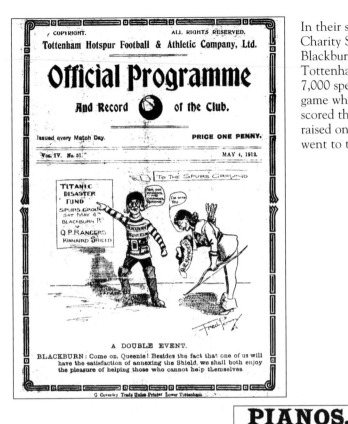

The team line-up for the match. In the early part of the century the Charity Shield had some of the trappings of today's cup final. At this time the Football League was predominately based in the North and the Shield offered an opportunity to show that there were good teams outside of the Football League playing in the Southern League. Alas, it was not to be Rangers' day.

The team for the 1913/14 season. Left to right, back row: Fielding, Saltwell, Wilson, Wilde, Jefferies, Matthews, Stephenson, Hart, Elliott, Keech (trainer). Third row: Draper, Whyman, Pennifer, Higgins, Wingrove, Nicholls, Pullen, Draper, Butler, A. Thompson, Cowan (manager). Second row: Ovens, Gregory, W. Thompson, Birch, Mitchell, Wake, Strugnell, Ingham, Fortune. Front row: Broster, Miller, Ives. The team finished eighth with a record of played 38, won 16, drawn 9 and lost 13 with a total of 41 points. They scored 45 goals and conceded 43.

In the 1913/14 season, Rangers were in mid-table for most of the campaign but saved their best performances for the FA Cup. Beating Bristol City away after a replay, they won further rounds away against Swansea Town and Birmingham City. The draw for the quarter-finals was again unkind, giving them a fixture away to Liverpool. The game went Liverpool's way in the early stages and they moved into a 2-0 lead. Rangers fought back and won two penalties. The first one was missed by Birch but the second was converted by Mitchell. Liverpool hung on to win 2-1 and ultimately proceeded to the final.

LIVERPOOL v. QUEENS PARK R.

At Anfield.   Kick-off 3-30 p.m.

Right.   1   Left.
Campbell

2   3
Longworth   Pursell or Speakman

4   5   6
Fairfoul   Lowe   Ferguson
         or Ferguson   or McKinlay

7   8   10   11
Sheldon Metcalf   Lacey   Nicholl

9
Miller

◯

Miller
14

Fortune   Gregory   Birch   Thompson
12   13   15   16

Wake   Mitchell   Whyman
17   18   19

Pullen   Ovens
20   21

Nicholls
Left.   22   Right.

Referee—Mr. G. H. Moody.
Linesmen—Messrs. J. W. Wright and C. H. Norton.

James Cowan resigned in 1914 to return to his native Scotland. He had been a most successful manager and the board appointed James Howie, another Scot, to take over. He had one full season before the First World War led to a makeshift London club programme which curtailed his opportunities. Howie resigned shortly before QPR joined the Football League in 1920.

The Southern League professional era had started with the raising of £5,000 to fund operations. The 1916/17 balance sheet tells the financial story of the club staying afloat via loans from the directors, support from the Railway Co. and from the bank manager. Even the players seem to be assisting!

Profit and Loss Account for Season ending 30th April, 1917.

1917. April 30th.						£	s.	d.	1917. April 30th.						£	s.	d.
To Match Expenses	...	...	...	...	...	537	5	4	By Gate Receipts	...	...	...	...	...	813	7	1
,, Repairs	...	...	...	...	...	8	5	10	,, Balance, being Net Loss for Season ending 30th April, 1917	...	...	...	...	29	12	1
,, Interest and Bank Charges	...	...	...	109	6	6									
,, Printing and Stationery	...	...	...	32	1	6									
,, League Subscription	...	...	...	4	4	0									
,, Insurance	...	...	...	...	...	11	0	0									
,, Postage and Sundries	...	...	...	11	14	4									
,, Rent	...	...	...	...	...	91	11	0									
,, Advertising	...	...	...	...	18	14	0									
,, London Combination	...	...	...	18	16	8									
						£842	19	2							£842	19	2

Balance Sheet, Season ending 1917.

LIABILITIES.			£	s.	d.	£	s.	d.	ASSETS.				£	s.	d.	£	s.	d.
To Nominal Capital —10,000 shares at 10/- each	...	...	5000	0	0				By Debtors	...	...	...				50	0	0
,, Capital Subscribed	...	...				1093	0	0	,, Plant	...	...	...				20	0	0
,, Sundry Creditors	...	...				269	5	4	,, League Deposits	...	...				8	0	0
,, Great Western Railway Co.	...				2129	13	11	,, Petty Cash in hand	...				1	5	7
,, Loans	...	...	...				2982	13	8	,, Profit and Loss deficiency, 30th April, 1916	...	...	...	7823	16	0	
,, London City and Westminster Bank overdraft	...	...				685	8	9	Add:								
,, Players' deferred wages	...	...				772	15	0	Net Loss as per Profit and Loss Account for Season ending 30th April, 1917	...	29	12	1		7853	8	1
						£7932	13	8								£7932	13	8

Signed on behalf of the Board, pursuant to Section 113 (Sub-Section 3) of the Companies (Consolidation) Act, 1908.

Dated this 15th day of November, 1917.

A. HARGREAVES.
J. ELLIOTT.
} Directors.

The above Accounts, with detailed vouchers, have been checked, and in our opinion this Balance Sheet is properly drawn up so as to exhibit a true and correct statement of the affairs of the Company as shown by their books.

15th November, 1917.

H. E. CLEVERLY.
WILLIAM EARLEY.
} Auditors.

Two
The Football League
Between the Wars
1920-1939

1920/21: Ned Liddell appointed as manager. Finish third in the first season. Great win in FA Cup against Arsenal, who were ninth in First Division.

1921/22: Draw against Arsenal at Highbury in FA Cup, but lose the replay at Loftus Road.

1922/23: Reach the last eight of the FA Cup, losing 1-0 to Sheffield United.

1923/24: Finish bottom and apply for re-election.

1925/26: Finish bottom again with only 21 points. Liddell departs.

1926/27: New manager is Bob Hewison. Rangers forget to enter the FA Cup!

1927/28: George Goddard scores 37 goals – a club record.

1928/29: Lose to Guildford City in the FA Cup.

1930: Ground closed following crowd disturbance. Rangers play a League game at Highbury.

1931/32: Sign a contract to play at the White City for twenty-one years. Beat Leeds 3-1 in FA Cup in front of record attendance of 41,000.

1933/34: Cash crisis. Club goes back to Loftus Road.

1935/36: B. Birrell is appointed manager. Rangers lose to Margate in the FA Cup.

1937/38: Sign Reg Allen and Alf Ridyard and finish third.

1938/39: Sell Cheetham to offset debt. Sign Alec Stock. Bill Birrell resigns and Ted Vizard takes over.

1939/40: Three games played before League is suspended. War competition arranged.

After a short spell as manager of Southend, Ned Liddell took on the responsibility of managing the Rangers in their first few seasons of Football League action. His early signings did well for him, taking the team to third place in the first season, but he will be best remembered for his FA Cup successes.

The team that represented QPR in their first Football League season. Left to right, back row: J. Manning, J. Wingrove, F. Blackman, T. O'Brien, H. Middlemiss. Front row: E. Price, R. Faulkner, T. Cain, A. Mitchell, W. Smith, J. Gregory. The record for 1920/21 was played 42, won 22, drawn 9 and lost 11 with a total of 53 points. Goals for were 61, goals against 32.

Rangers' Edgeley closes in on Swindon Town 'keeper Skiller in the opening match of the 1921/22 season. The match result was a 0-0 draw.

Knight slides the winning goal past the Aberdare 'keeper Leahy on 12 November 1921. E. Knight was signed from local team Botwell Mission and made his debut in this game, scoring the winning goal. In spite of this grand start he only ever made one further appearance for the First XI!

QUEEN'S PARK RANGERS v. THE ARSENAL (1st Round English Cup).

QUEEN'S PARK RANGERS.

RIGHT WING

LEFT WING

Goal.

1...**Hill**

Backs.

2...**Wingrove**   3...**Grimsdell**

Half Backs.

4...**Grant**   5...**Mitchell**   6...**O'Brien**

Forwards.

7...**Manning**   8...**Birch**   9...**Smith**   10...**Chandler**   11...**Gregory**

Referee—Mr. C. AUSTIN.

Goals.
A. Pts.
17 29
—   29
v   28
7   28
6   29

Next Match,
X Div. POLICE.
(Friendly)
Saturday next   Kick-off 2.45

LEFT WING

RIGHT WING

12...**Dr. J. A. Paterson** 13...**Blyth** 14...**Pagnam**   15...**White**   16...**Rutherford**

Forwards.

17...**McKinnon**   18...**Graham**   19...**Baker**

Half-Backs.

20...**Hutchins**   21...**Shaw**

Backs.

THE ARSENAL.   22...**Williamson**

Goal.

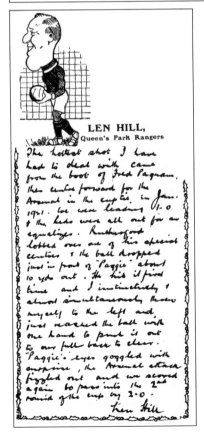

LEN HILL,
Queen's Park Rangers

One of QPR's great victories. This is the programme for the first round FA Cup-tie played at Loftus Road on 8 January 1921. Arsenal finished ninth in Division One that season but on this day Division Three Rangers were the top dogs, winning 2-0.

Len Hill, the Rangers goalkeeper of the day, has his memories of that special match. He wrote: 'The hottest shot I have had to deal with came from the boot of Fred Pagnam, the centre forward for the Arsenal in the cup tie in Jan. 1921. We were leading 1-0 and the Reds were all out for an equaliser. Rutherford lobbed over one of his special centres and the ball dropped just in front of "Paggie" about 10 yds out. He hit it first time and I instinctively and almost simultaneously threw myself to the left and just reached the ball with one hand to punch it out to our full back to clear. "Paggies'" eyes goggled with surprise, the Arsenal attack fizzled out and we scored again to pass into the 2nd round of the cup by 2-0.'

32

Arthur Chandler, scorer of one of the goals in that famous cup-tie, joined Rangers in 1920 from local club Hempstead at the age of twenty-four and played well over his three seasons. He scored 18 goals in his 86 games but when he went on to Leicester City for a £3,000 transfer fee, he really blossomed and became their record striker with a total of 273 goals.

Len Hill, Rangers' famous goalie. Despite severe head injuries resulting from action with the 9th Lancers during the First World War, he proved himself a top goalkeeper, making 176 appearances for the club, having been signed from Southend United in 1920. He was first choice custodian until his transfer to Southampton in 1925.

 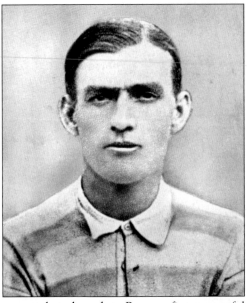

Grant (left) and Smith were two fine players who contributed much to Rangers first successful season in the Football League, both playing in every game in the 1920/21 campaign. Both, however, left the club toward the end of the following season.

TEAMS FOR SATURDAY, JANUARY 7th. 1922

R   **ARSENAL**   L

Williamson
1

Bradshaw   Hutchins
2   3

Milne   Graham   Whittaker
4   5   6

Rutherford   Blyth   White   A. Goodman   Toner
7   8   9   10   11

O

Gregory   Chandler   Smith   Birch   Edgley
12   13   14   15   16

Burnham   O'Brien   Grant
17   18   19

Bain   Marsden
20   21

Hill
22

L   **QUEEN'S PARK RANGERS**   R

Referee—Mr. T. L. BEELEY (Sheffield).
Linesmen—Messrs. F. H. WALL (London) & S. SYMS (Kent).

For the second season in succession QPR played Arsenal in the FA Cup, this time at Highbury, and here Arsenal were well set to gain their revenge for the previous season's defeat. For manager Ned Liddell these cup matches were to stretch his loyalties as he spent some years with the Gunners in his playing days. Rangers acquitted themselves well in getting a 0-0 draw at Highbury, but lost the midweek replay at Loftus Rd 1-2.

Long-serving Rangers trainer Wally Draper takes players John, Pournham, Bain, Watson and goalkeeper Hill through their exercises during pre-season training for the 1922/23 season. However, they seem more interested in the camera!

The efforts of Draper the trainer seemed to have had a good effect as QPR went through to the quarter-finals of the FA Cup. On the way they defeated Crystal Palace and South Shields at Loftus Road and Wigan Borough away. Shown here on the later trip it appears that the team might well have landed the first hat sponsorship!

The welcome mat was out for these twelve new players at the start of the 1923/24 season – but it was quantity not quality that arrived! Left to right: H. Dobinson, C.R. Cooper, L.S. Waugh, S.W. Abbot, J.N. Mason, W. Hurst, W. Pierce, J. Cameron, T. Allison, G. Hart, J.S. Keen, G.H. Benson. The team finished bottom and had to apply for re-election for the first time in its Football League history.

A feature of many football clubs' programmes during the 1920s and '30s was the front cover cartoon. QPR reserves appear in this one; its not only football that has changed, so has humour! Reserve team matches were well attended in the early days as the opportunity to travel was both difficult and expensive for the average fan. There was no results service available to fans until the six o'clock radio bulletin, so a visit to the reserve match was an alternative.

The 1924/25 team was, from left to right, back row: Pierce, Knowles, Hill (standing), Birch, Harris, Ogley. Front row: Brown, John, Johnson, Moore, Bolam. The team's record for the season was played 42, won 14, drawn 8 and lost 20 with a total of 36 points. They scored 42 goals but let in 63. The showing was only a marginal improvement on the previous year's performance, being just four places off the bottom. As a result the manager, Ned Liddell, left the club to be replaced by Bob Hewison and, initially, he struggled too.

Bob Hewison came to Rangers after his first spell of management at Northampton Town. His first season saw QPR back at the foot of the Third Division and again applying for re-election, but he did get QPR playing in the famous blue and white hoops and he also signed the all-time record goalscorer George Goddard.

Jimmy Birch was a great creative player who would be in any QPR hall of fame collection. He made 363 appearances as the playmaker for the team but still managed 144 goals during his Rangers career that spanned 1912 to 1926. This fine record takes into account the fact that he missed five seasons as a result of the First World War.

Bill Pierce joined Rangers as a sixteen year old from the north-east and played 193 games over his 8 seasons. His reputation was as a traditional full-back – fortunately he played when the sliding tackle was admired! He transferred to Carlisle United in 1931.

Detail of a pre-season tour in Turkey during the mid-to-late-twenties has not been recorded, but the team and coaching staff seem to be enjoying the touring scenario! This photograph was taken at the team's hotel.

Woodward, Arrowsmith and Armstrong report for pre-season training in 1928/29. The background in this photograph is the old Elleslie Road Stand, which at that time housed both the club executive rooms and the player dressing rooms.

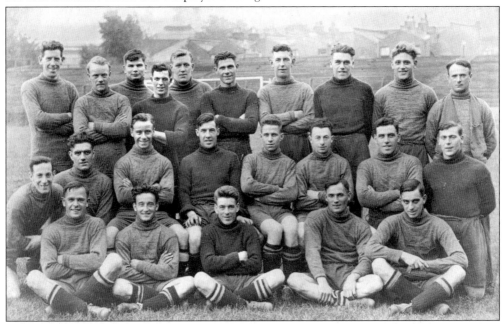

This 1928/29 side finished sixth in Division Three and were only three points off being champions! They lost only nine games during the season, two less than the champions Charlton Athletic. Left to right, back row: McNab, Neil, Mason, Wiles, Cockburn, Whatmore, Cunningham, Armstrong, Nixon, Mayson (trainer). Middle row: Harris, Eggleton, Coward, Evans, Rounce, Young, Pierce, Groome. Front row: Goddard, Rogers, Moffatt, Foster, Yates. QPR's record for this season was played 42, won 19, drawn 14 and lost 9, and they amassed 52 points. They scored 82 goals and conceded 61.

Bob Hewison, manager of this 1929/30 team, was due to see some results from his efforts of the past four years and this side gave him that encouragement. They finished third, equalling Rangers best performance since joining the Third Division. This effort was spearheaded by George Goddard who netted a club record 37 goals in the season. From left to right, standing: Mason (trainer), Armstrong, Cunningham, Nixon, Halton, Whatmore, Sales. Kneeling: Legge, Pierce, Rounce, Goddard, Howe. Their record was played 42, won 21, drawn 9 and lost 12 with 51 points. They netted 80 goals and conceded 64.

In 1931/32 Rangers were mid-table for most of the season but they preformed well in the FA Cup, reaching the fourth round. After defeating Barnet and Scunthorpe United they were drawn at home to Leeds United in the third round. A record crowd of 41,097 spectators turned up at the White City ground to see Rangers outplay the top Second Division side, winning 3-1. In this QPR attack, Potts, the Leeds United goalkeeper, punches clear watched by Rounce, Ranger's inside forward. Danskin covers for Leeds.

QUEEN'S PARK RANGERS

FOOTBALL CLUB

Souvenir of the Visit of
FIRST VIENNA CLUB
(AUSTRIA)
MONDAY. 30TH JANUARY. 1933

WHITE CITY STADIUM
WOOD LANE · W·12

Printed and Published for the Club by
F. E. Blower & Co. Sutton Road Works. Watford

OFFICIAL PROGRAMME ~ 2ᴰ

The move to the White City in 1931 had been undertaken to build the gate and the status of the club, but by 1933 the financial position was deteriorating. A number of efforts were made to address the situation, one of which was to stage a match against the top Austrian side, First Vienna.

Representatives of the Austrian Government meet the players before the match. From left to right: Armstrong, Barrie, Goodier, H. Wyles, Collins, J. Hill.

George Goddard is an obvious choice as a hall of fame Ranger. To this day he holds the club's goalscoring record of 189 netted over 259 appearances, including 15 hat-tricks in his 8 seasons with the club. Signed from non-League Redhill in the summer of 1926, he was eventually transferred in September 1933 to Brentford.

FIRST PUBLIC EXPERIMENTAL **FLOODLIGHT MATCH** BETWEEN SELECTED LONDON TEAMS

S (Red Shirts and White Knickers)

Goalkeeper
1. EMERY
(Clapton Orient)

White Balls will be

	Right Back		Left Back	
	2. FRENCH		3. SWEETMAN	
	(Brentford)		(Millwall)	
Right Half-Back		Centre Half-Back		Left Half-Back
4. TOMKINS		5. GOODIER		6. WOODWARD
(Fulham)		(Q. P. Rangers)		(Watford)
Outside Right	Inside Right	Centre Forward	Inside Left	Outside Left
HORTON	8. BLACK	9. GODDARD	10. HARKINS	11. CLARK
(Charlton A.)	(Charlton A.)	(Q. P. Rangers)	(Millwall)	(Crystal Palace)

Referee :—
A. J. JEWELL

Linesmen :—
H. E. McGregor & D. M. Griffiths

Outside Left	Inside Left	Centre Forward	Inside Right	Outside Right
RUFFELL	13. DUDLEY	14. LAMBERT	15. BRAIN	16. REED
(West Ham)	(Chelsea)	(Arsenal)	(Tottenham H.)	(Arsenal)
	Left Half-Back	Centre Half-Back		Right Half-Back
	17. JOHNSON	18. HAYNES		19. EVANS
	(West Ham)	(Arsenal)		(Tottenham H.)
		Left Back	Right Back	
		20. BARBER	21. FRYATT	
		(Chelsea)	(West Ham)	

TES (White Shirts & Black Knickers)

Goalkeeper
22. PREEDY
(Arsenal)

Kick off

Floodlit football in the early 1930s was strictly prohibited, but the London clubs wished to assess its possibilities and the following request was forwarded to the FA: 'This conference of the London and Watford league clubs asks the FA to sanction a match by artificial light at the White City'. As a one-off concession this was agreed – to be organised by QPR. It would be around twenty years before the FA formally agreed to floodlit football.

43

QUEEN'S PARK RANGERS
Football and Athletic Club, Ltd.

Directors' Announcement.

Our Manager, Mr. A. P. Mitchell, has tendered his resignation to take effect at the end of this season. The Directors have accepted it and wish Mr. Mitchell every success in any future position he may undertake. Mr. Mitchell has, over a great number of years, rendered very valuable services to the Club both as a player and later as a Manager, and the Directors wish to place on record their appreciation of these services.

The Price for Season Tickets next season at Loftus Road has been fixed at £3. 7s. 6d. but, if purchased before the 1st June, 1933, the price will be reduced to £3. Special Reserved accommodation in the Centre Stand will be provided and it will greatly assist the Club if our present Season Ticket holders will make their application early. Many more such holders are required and this is just another way in which you can give practical help.

The Directors are very concerned with the serious financial position of the Club and an urgent appeal is made to our supporters, and their friends, to attend every home match for the remainder of the Season. Every penny in gate money is urgently needed—we are heavily in debt due to the poor support received at our Home matches for the past three or four months. The Directors have been fully alive to the poor display of the team but, unfortunately, without money, new Players to strengthen the weak spots cannot be obtained.

The Directors have dug, and are digging, deeply into their pockets to keep the Club alive but unless there is better support given between now and the end of the Season, it will be extremely difficult for the Club to carry on next year. Unfortunately, the Directors' enterprise in staging Football at the White City has proved a failure and heavy financial losses have been made ; therefore, there was no alternative but to terminate the Agreement with the White City Stadium. The Directors are willing to still further financially assist the Club during the difficult times we are going through, provided more of our Supporters apply for Shares. The pre-

vious appeals have brought forward quite a fair response but if we are to continue next Season, then a large sum of money is required for Summer wages and the acquisition of new Players, therefore many more applications are required.

Now you Supporters, rally round the old Club by sending forward your application for Shares without delay. Instalments will be gladly accepted. Such an investment should ultimately prove beneficial. It is obvious we have a loyal band of supporters by the number of faces regularly seen at all our Home matches. Will that loyal band canvas for further support in a tangible form? The following are the ways you can assist the Club :

1. Applying for Shares.
2. Attending all the remaining Home matches.
3. Inducing all your friends to do likewise.
4. Buying a programme.
5. Supporting Mr. Evemy by buying tickets for the "Penny-on-the-Ball" competition.
6. Purchasing a Season Ticket before 1st June.

I am permitted to say that our Chairman—Mr. C. W. Fielding—has again come forward with very generous financial support. This is in addition to the very large sum of money advanced by him in days gone by and which is still unpaid. The Club is lucky to have such a generous sportsman at its head. Other Directors have also promised to financially assist but naturally there is a limit to their generous help. It is now up to us all to support the Chairman and his Co-Directors to the very best of our ability.

From the number of letters received it is very evident that our return to the Loftus Road ground next Season is popular. Can we survive until then? It is now up to you, Mr. Supporter !

Remember, a first-class side cannot be built up and maintained without good and consistent support from the Public. The successful Club is the one well supported, win or lose, wet or fine.

There was another financial crisis as the move to the White City had failed, so the club moved back to Loftus Road for the 1933/34 season. The directors issued this appeal for support.

With the new season (1933/34) came a new manager. Mick O'Brien, an ex-Ireland international and a player for the club in the early twenties, was appointed. While most managers get photographed with their new team, O'Brien chose to appear among the club's back-up staff. Left to right, back row: W. Goodman (groundsman), J. Denoon (maintenance), D. Richards (trainer). Front row: J. Eggleton (assistant trainer), M.T. O'Brien, G. Hurley (office), the manager's dog.

The QPR team that O'Brien moulded took the club to the third round of the FA Cup in the 1933/34 season and up to their highest position yet of fourth in the Third Division (South). Left to right, back row: Barrie, March, Goodier, Beecham, Ashman, Blake. Front row: Emmerson, Eaton, Blackman, Devine, Brown. The team's record was played 42, won 24, drawn 6 and lost 12 with 54 points. They scored 70 goals and conceded 51. The following season, the team fell back to the bottom half of the table and O'Brien moved on to become assistant manager at Brentford.

The 1935/36 season saw another change, with Billy Birrell coming in as manager, and things certainly changed for the better. Leading up to the Second World War, his teams finished fourth, ninth, third and sixth in successive years, which for Rangers was their best run since joining the Football League.

The outstanding signing of Birrell's regime was that of Tommy Cheetham in 1936, formerly of India and the Army. Cheetham was always up front in the team's successes. He scored 92 goals in his 128 appearances, which was a very high goals to games ratio. In March 1939 he was transferred to Brentford for £5,000, which was useful income to the cash-strapped club and helped QPR through some of the early problems of running football during the war.

The 1936/37 team was, from left to right, back row: Cheetham, Carr, Allan, Moralee, Ballantyn. Third row: Royan, Richards (trainer), Swinfen, Bartlett, Mason, W. Mason, J. Barrie, Farmer, Eggleton (assistant trainer), Fitzgerald. Second row: Jefferson, Lowe, Lumsden, W. Birrell (manager), Abel, Cameron, Rowe. Front row: Crawford, Clark, March, McMahon, Vincent, Bott. QPR's record for that season was played 42, won 18, drawn 9 and lost 15 with 45 points. The team netted 73 times and conceded 52.

When he joined QPR in 1938, Alec Stock had no thought that much of his future success would be associated with the club. It was not his 56 appearances that were to influence his career, but his later role as a highly respected manager who would make Rangers the first Division Three side to play in a Wembley cup final.

Allen, Rangers' young goalkeeper, takes this cross and prevents Watford's Dunderdale and Evans from connecting. James, Howe and Jefferson cover for QPR, who lost this match 1-4 on 17 December 1938. Reg Allen was called up for service early in 1940 and was taken prisoner shortly afterwards. Released in 1944, he picked up his career again with Rangers and was quickly recognised as a fine goalkeeper.

Before the Second World War the London Challenge Cup was a major first team prize for the London clubs. Rangers had only won this cup once until this team gave QPR its second victory in 1938/39. All the signs were that Billy Birrell was building a side that might at last take QPR into the Second Division. Alas, the war stopped that. Left to right, back row: Reay, Mason, Abel. Third row: Powell, Ridyard, Farmer. Second row: Pearson, Warburton, McEwan, McCarthy, Pattison. Front row: Wodehouse (chairman), Eggleton (trainer).

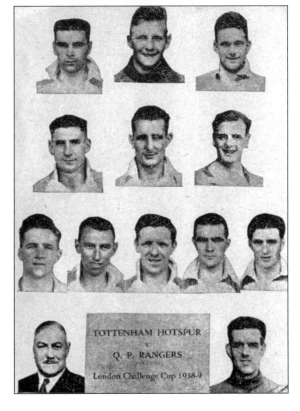

Three

War, Peace and Promotion 1939-1964

1939/40: Rangers play in the emergency war leagues set up on a regional basis. They play in two competitions, finishing first and second respectively. All players' contracts are suspended for the duration of the war.

1940-42: Club play in various London/Southern competitions. Guest players were allowed.

1942/43: Rangers use thirty-three players (including eight guests) and reach the semi-final of the League South Cup.

1943/44: Ted Vizard resigns. Dave Mangnall takes over as manager.

1946/47: Back to Third Division football. The club miss promotion but attain their highest Division Three position, finishing second to Cardiff City. Another cash crisis. A total of £45,000 is raised by issue of new share capital.

1947/48: Champions of Division Three (South) and promoted to the Second Division for first time in their history. Reach the fifth round of the FA Cup.

1948/49: Finish thirteenth in first season in the Second Division, the best League position they were to attain under Mangnall.

1951/52: Relegated in 1952. Dave Mangnall resigns.

1953: First west London club to install floodlights. Jack Taylor becomes manager.

1959: Alec Stock becomes manager and results improve.

1960/61: Placed third in Division Three, the club's highest position for nine years.

1962: Another failed attempt to move to White City.

1963: John Bloom, the washing machine entrepreneur, tries to take over the club.

1964: Jim Gregory arrives.

The Fielding family had been the major driving force at QPR since around 1907 and it was their bank guarantees and financial backing that had kept the club in business during the twenties and thirties. Charles Fielding, the chairman from 1929, saw the club through the war years and retired from the board in 1944.

Reg Swinfen was a versatile full-back, winger and centre forward, but his career was interrupted by the war. Including his wartime appearances he made 117 starts for the Rangers, scoring 42 goals.

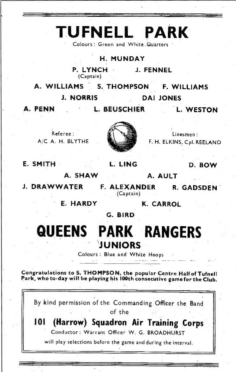

TUFNELL PARK
Colours: Green and White Quarters

H. MUNDAY

P. LYNCH J. FENNEL
(Captain)

A. WILLIAMS S. THOMPSON F. WILLIAMS

J. NORRIS DAI JONES

A. PENN L. BEUSCHIER L. WESTON

Referee: Linesmen:
A/C A. H. BLYTHE F. H. ELKINS, Cpl. REELAND

E. SMITH L. LING D. BOW

A. SHAW A. AULT

J. DRAWWATER F. ALEXANDER R. GADSDEN
(Captain)

E. HARDY K. CARROL

G. BIRD

QUEENS PARK RANGERS
JUNIORS
Colours: Blue and White Hoops

Congratulations to S. THOMPSON, the popular Centre Half of Tufnell Park, who to-day will be playing his 100th consecutive game for the Club.

By kind permission of the Commanding Officer the Band
of the
101 (Harrow) Squadron Air Training Corps
Conductor: Warrant Officer W. G. BROADHURST
will play selections before the game and during the interval.

Ted Vizard (above left) came to Rangers in 1939 following six years as the boss at Swindon Town. He never had the opportunity of building on the groundwork laid by Billy Birrell as his time was spent getting eleven players together each Saturday for every match in a war-torn Shepherds Bush. He left in 1944 to take the reins at Wolverhampton Wanderers. Vizard did however have one first while at QPR – Rangers initial appearance at Wembley in the Middlesex Senior Red Cross Cup final. Tufnell Park won by 3 goals to 2 and six of these junior players went on to make first team appearances. Ron Gadsden (right) was probably the best prospect but for the limitations imposed by the war. Gate money at the final raised £270 6s for charities.

CHELSEA FOOTBALL CLUB

Official Programme

SATURDAY APRIL 24th 1943 ·   PRICE ONE PENNY

ARSENAL v. QUEEN'S PARK RANGERS

FOOTBALL LEAGUE SOUTH   Kick-off 3 p.m.
Cup Competition
Semi - Final Tie   ARSENAL (Red)

MARKS
Goal

SCOTT   COMPTON (L.)
Right Back (2)   *Left Back (3)*

CRAYSTON   B. JOY   MALE (Capt.)
Right Half (4)   *Centre Half (5)*   *Left Half (6)*

BRISCOE   NELSON   LEWIS   BASTIN   COMPTON (D.)
Outside Right (7)   *Inside Right (8)*   *Centre (9)*   *Inside Left (10)*   *Outside Left (11)*

                   Mr. A. CURTIS
                      Red and White Flag
Referee—Mr. P. STEVENS (Luton)   *Linesmen*   Mr. W. C. REES
                      Blue and White Flag

PATTISON   BURLEY   W. HEATHCOTE   McEWAN   SWINFEN
Outside Left (11)   *Inside Left (10)*   *Centre (9)*   *Inside Right (8)*   *Outside Right (7)*

MALLETT   RIDYARD (Capt.)   SMITH
Left Half (6)   *Centre Half (5)*   *Right Half (4)*

ABEL   ROSE
Left Back (3)   *Right Back (2)*

BROWN
Goal

QUEEN'S PARK RANGERS (Blue and White)

WELCOME   To-day we extend a hearty welcome to our friends from Highbury and Shepherd's Bush. Both have well earned a place in to-day's Semi-Final and each are no doubt confident of their ability to win and thus qualify for a place in the Final at Wembley on Saturday next. Chelsea followers will be able to sit back and enjoy the feast, and will no doubt join with us in wishing " May the best team win."

AIR RAID WARNING—In the event of an Air Raid Warning the Ground exits will be opened, so that those who wish to leave can do so. Play will proceed unless the " Spotter " reports enemy activity in the vicinity.

Trussells, London.

MONDAY NEXT at 3.15 p.m.
Inter-Allied Services Cup-Final
BRITISH ARMY v. R.A.F.
Preceded at 2 p.m. by
NORWEGIAN ARMY v. BELGIAN ARMY.

THE METROPOLITAN POLICE CENTRAL BAND
By kind permission of the Commissioner of Police for the Metropolis
will render Musical Selections.
Conductor: Flight-Lieut. J. H. AMERS, M.B.E., P.S.M.

The Football League South Cup semi-final at Stamford Bridge, with QPR ninety minutes away from a first senior Wembley visit. The Arsenal team, which was littered with international stars, proved their quality by decisively defeating the R's 4-1. Pattison (below) scored Rangers goal in front of a crowd of 54,000.

TOWN v. QUEEN'S PARK RANGERS (Football League South)

RIGHT]   **"TOWN"** (Red and Blue)   5-2-44   [LEFT

BRIGGS (Halifax)

2 HORTON   **3 ROYSTON** (Plymouth)

4 BRITTON (Everton)   **5 CULLIS** (Wolves)   **6 MERCER** (Everton)

7 WHITE   **8 MORRIS**   **9 THOMAS**   **10 TRIGG**   **11 CUNLIFFE**
(Preston N.E.)   (Stockport)   (Fulham)   (Bradford City)   (Hull City)

TRIGG   *WATSON*

NEXT HOME MATCH

BRENTFORD

Saturday, February 12th

Kick Off 3.0 p.m.

Referee:
G. READER

Linesmen:
W. G. BREEZE—Red Flag
H. C. BAUGH—Blue Flag

Kick Off 3.0 p.m.

11 BURLEY   **10 SOMERFIELD**   **9 HEATHCOTE**   **8 LOWES**   **7 LITTLE**

6 MALLETT   **5 RIDYARD**   **4 SMITH**

3 ABEL   **2 ROSE**

BROWN

LEFT]   **Q.P. RANGERS** (White Knickers, Blue & White Hoops Shirts) [RIGHT

With the massive army unit based at Aldershot, it was common during the war that their team would include many international guest players. On 5 February 1944 Rangers found themselves playing against the England half-back line of Britton, Cullis and Mercer (below, left to right) and they still came away with a 3-1 win.

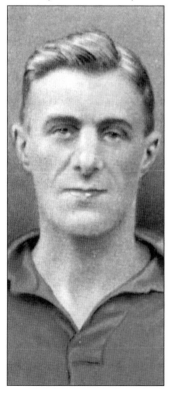  

53

When Ted Vizard moved on to Wolves in 1944 the club turned to Dave Mangnall (above left and right) to improve their fortunes. He had spent most of his early football days in the north of England before coming to London in 1935. He played in the capital for West Ham and Millwall prior to his signing for QPR in May 1939. After playing virtually all his 131 games for Rangers in the wartime leagues he was appointed the club manager in April 1944. He quickly adapted from hooped shirt to dark suit and could lay claim to having the best managerial record in the history of the club up to that time.

Wilf Heathcote was a great favourite of the wartime fans and a major contributor to the good performances during the war seasons. His strike rate was tremendous, scoring 90 times in 105 appearances, but he moved on to Millwall at the end of the war and soon faded out of League football.

In April 1946 the Rangers went off to Germany to take on the British Army of the Rhine in Hamburg. Alighting from the plane are Daniels, McEwan, Ridyard, Addinall, Mangnall (looking for a game of golf?), Jack Rose and Bert Baker (director).

The team leaves the airport in relaxed mood unaware that a 0-5 defeat awaited them! Left to right, back row: Ridyard, Allen, Rose, Eggleton, McEwan. Middle row: Wodehouse (director), Chapman, Pattison, Daniels, Addinall, Mallett. Front row: Baker (director), Heath, Hittinger (chairman), Mangnall (manager).

The backroom staff that supported the 1947/48 title winning side. Left to right, back row: March (catering), McCarthy (ground staff), Ridyard (coach), Harris (office), Butterworth (groundsman). Front row: Hittinger (director), Hurley (secretary), Mangnall (manager), Eggleton (trainer).

The boys at the back in 1947/48. Left to right, back row: Jefferson, Rose, Reay. Front row: Saphin, Swinfen, Allen.

The midfielders. Back row: Daniels, Blizzard, Barr, Powell. Front row: Smith, Ridyard, Heath.

The goal-getters. Back row: McEwan, Neary, Mallett, Whitehead. Front row: Parkinson, Armitage, Pattison. As Division Three champions, Queens Park Rangers were at last going up to the Second Division after twenty-eight years of trying. Their record was played 42, won 26, drawn 9 and lost 7 with 61 points. The team netted 74 goals and conceded exactly half that number.

INTRODUCED BY THE SUPPORTERS' CLUB.

THE QUEEN'S PARK RANGERS FOOTBALL AND ATHLETIC CLUB
LIMITED.

Registered Office:—ELLERSLIE ROAD, SHEPHERDS BUSH, LONDON, W.12.

SHARE CAPITAL - £45,000

divided into 30,000 5% Redeemable Cumulative Preference Shares of £1 each and 30,000 Ordinary Shares of 10/- each.

ISSUE OF

20,000 5% REDEEMABLE CUMULATIVE PREFERENCE SHARES OF £1 EACH AT PAR AND 20,000 ORDINARY SHARES OF 10/- EACH AT PAR.

	5% Redeemable Cumulative Pref. Shares of £1 each.	Ordinary Shares of 10/- each
Payable on Application	10/- per share	5/- per share
Payable on Allotment	10/- ,, ,,	5/- ,, ,,
	20/- ,, ,,	10/- ,, ,,

FORM OF APPLICATION FOR SHARES.

Cash problems re-emerged and the club were forced to go to the market again for a further £45,000, which was required to consolidate their Second Division status and pay for urgent ground improvements.

This photograph shows how the money was needed! On Saturday 7 February 1948 during the fifth round FA Cup-tie there were 30,000 fans packed into the ground when a section of the terrace fencing collapsed. Police and ambulancemen were soon on the scene and a major disaster was averted. It got better as Rangers won the match 3-1.

Fred Durrant was a typical old-time centre forward who was signed in September 1946 from Brentford. He played in the promotion challenge of 1946/47 and the promotion winning side the following year. While appearing in only 53 games, his 26 goals over the two years were vital to QPR's success.

In the midst of their drive for Second Division status Rangers went on their best FA Cup run for many years. They reached the sixth round and were drawn against the 1946 FA Cup winners Derby County, a star-studded Division One side. The result hinged on this hotly disputed goal that earned Derby a replay at the Baseball Ground. This picture shows the look of despair on Reg Allen's face while Arthur Jefferson looks toward the referee for a decision he did not get. With only nine fit men on the field, due to injury, QPR lost the replay 5-0.

McDonald Bailey needed to tune up for the 100 meters in the forthcoming Olympic Games and Rangers needed to be sharp for their promotion push so manager Dave Mangnall got them training together at Loftus Road. McEwan and Durrant seem happier to talk than chase the sprinter!

The 1947/48 championship team that gained Second Division status for Queens Park Rangers for the first time since they entered the Football League in the 1919/20 season. Left to right, back row: Eggleton (trainer), I. Powell, G. Powell, Allen, A. Smith, Addinall, Jefferson, Dave Mangnall (manager). Front row: McEwan, Hatton, G. Smith, Mills, Hartburn. There was a lot of talent in this team, but while Ivor Powell, Reg Allen ,Geo Smith, Cyril Hatton and Don Mills may have been the stars, winning the championship was essentially a team performance and a lot of the credit for that must go to Dave Mangnall the manager.

In July 1948 the long-suffering supporters celebrated the team's achievement with a gala dinner. Dave Mangnall is in attendance with the Championship Shield. Some of the people attending had supported the club for over twenty years and the night was one of nostalgia and of excitement for the coming season.

This success made Dave Mangnall a man in demand and he is seen here in talks with film star Mai Zetterling when the team members were invited to the Lime Grove Studios to celebrate their successful season. Team members include: Durrant, McEwan, G. Powell, Addinall, Ramscar, Mangnall, I. Powell.

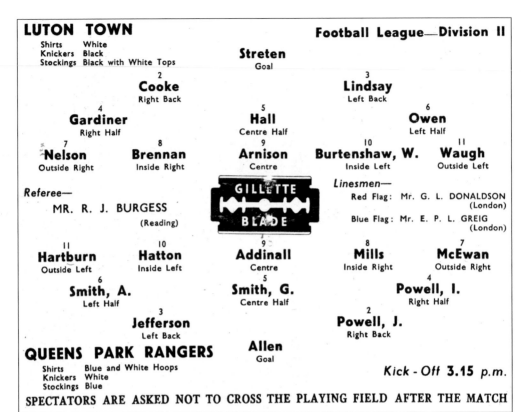

LUTON TOWN

Shirts   White
Knickers Black
Stockings Black with White Tops

Football League—Division II

Streten
Goal

2
Cooke
Right Back

3
Lindsay
Left Back

4
Gardiner
Right Half

5
Hall
Centre Half

6
Owen
Left Half

7
Nelson
Outside Right

8
Brennan
Inside Right

9
Arnison
Centre

10
Burtenshaw, W.
Inside Left

11
Waugh
Outside Left

Referee—
MR. R. J. BURGESS
(Reading)

Linesmen—
Red Flag: Mr. G. L. DONALDSON
(London)
Blue Flag: Mr. E. P. L. GREIG
(London)

11
Hartburn
Outside Left

10
Hatton
Inside Left

9
Addinall
Centre

8
Mills
Inside Right

7
McEwan
Outside Right

6
Smith, A.
Left Half

5
Smith, G.
Centre Half

4
Powell, I.
Right Half

3
Jefferson
Left Back

2
Powell, J.
Right Back

QUEENS PARK RANGERS

Allen
Goal

Shirts   Blue and White Hoops
Knickers White
Stockings Blue

Kick - Off 3.15 p.m.

SPECTATORS ARE ASKED NOT TO CROSS THE PLAYING FIELD AFTER THE MATCH

The programme for Rangers first Second Division game away to Luton Town on 21 August 1948. The game finished 0-0 and, as three wins followed, Rangers went to the top of Division Two by the end of August. While the team did not maintain those heady heights, they finished the season in thirteenth and felt they had consolidated the club's progress.

Reg Allen comes out to prevent Monk of Brentford from scoring, while George Powell covers during this game on 9 October 1948. This was the first time since the 1932/33 season that these local rivals had met in a traditional League game. Rangers won 2-0 with Hudson and Hartburn scoring.

Cyril Hatton was a vital member of the QPR sides immediately after the war. He had good talent on the ball and was the playmaker of the side. In his eight seasons with the club he made 208 starts, scoring 87 goals. This picture has him mixing it with Lincoln's Johnson and goalkeeper Moulson during the 2-0 win at Loftus Road in November 1948.

When the 1948/49 season ended the team went off on a tour of Turkey for the second year running, where there played three games. The line-up for this pre-match team photograph was, from left to right, back row: unknown, Parkinson, Reay, Mangnall, Chapman, Saphin, Eggleton, Nicholas, Heath, Baker. Front row: Muir, Duggan, Stewart, Farrow, Wardle. The Turk on the front row is unknown.

With the 1949/50 season approaching, the hard work is not just on the training pitch! New signing Horace Woodward checks the uprights while Billy Pointon pulls the strings.

On 7 September 1949 Preston North End were the visitors to Loftus Road. There was an intriguing personal duel between old Rangers favourite Arthur Jefferson and England's star winger Tom Finney. This fairly contested confrontation ended equal, as did the match with the result being 0-0.

Reg Allen made his debut for QPR in November 1938. When the war came he was one of the first to sign on and ultimately he joined the parachute regiment. Captured in Italy, he spent most of the war in German prison camps. In 1946 he restarted his Rangers career and was quickly recognised as one of the outstanding 'keepers in the Football League. He made 251 appearances for the Rs and a number of the top clubs made enquiries about him. In June 1950 he moved to Manchester United for £10,000 – a world record fee for a goalkeeper!

The 1950/51 campaign gets under way with new signings Shepherd and Waugh. Left to right, back row: Nelson, Mills, Saphin, G. Powell, Heath, Woodward. Front row: Waugh, Stewart, Addinall, Shepherd, Farrow. It was a tough season but Rangers were never in relegation problems. The team finished in sixteenth position and their record was played 42, won 15, drawn 10 and lost 17 with 40 points. They scored 71 and conceded 82 goals.

One signing that did not make the starting line up for the first game of the season in August 1950 was Tony Ingham, who joined in June 1950 from Leeds United. He did not need to worry as, following his club debut in November, he went on to make a record 548 appearances for Rangers, including five consecutive seasons as an ever-present. After finishing his playing career he has served the club as an administrator, temporary secretary and in more recent years as a director of the club, and he still travels to all away games. Who said club loyalty had died?

Over the years the club have always had a strong supporters' club and they produced virtually all the post-war handbooks that provide a nostalgic view of past seasons. The 1951 committee is shown here.

The Supporters' Club cycling section leave the old Ellerslie Road entrance, off on a Sunday morning spin which gives them the opportunity to relive the previous day's game.

Dave Mangnall's spell as manager came to an end following relegation in 1952. He was followed by Jack Taylor, who is being welcomed here as Rangers' new boss by chairman Hittinger in May 1952. His previous experience in charge was somewhat limited as his first and only prior position was as player-manager of Weymouth. His seven years in charge of QPR were unexciting and the highest Division Three place achieved was tenth in 1957 and 1958.

The squad that Jack Taylor inherited contained a few recent signings, but the 1952/53 team struggled and finished twenty-first out of twenty-four teams. Left to right, back row: Hold, Powell, Heath, Ingham. Middle row: Poppitt, Clayton, Brown, Gullan, Chapman, Hill. Front row: Waugh, Stewart, Muir, Gilberg, Spence, Addinall, Smith, Hatton, Shepherd. The team had the record of played 46, won 12, drawn 15 and lost 19 with 39 points. They scored 61 goals, but conceded 82.

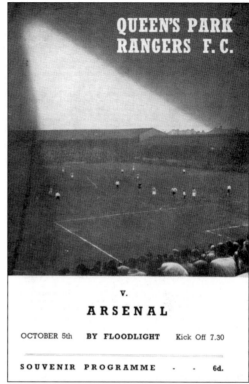

The highlight of the 1953/54 season was the switching on of the newly installed floodlights in October. QPR were the first team in West London to get lights and Arsenal were invited to Loftus Road for the official switching on. An attendance of over 16,000 were at the ground to see Arsenal, who were fielding their full first team, win 3-1. Film star Pat Kirkwood accompanied Don Roper of Arsenal and Jim Taylor of QPR to the centre circle for the kick-off.

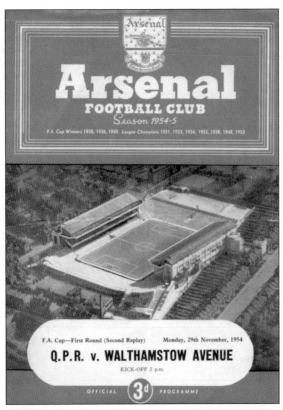

F.A. Cup—First Round (Second Replay)   Monday, 29th November, 1954

Q.P.R. v. WALTHAMSTOW AVENUE

KICK-OFF 2 p.m.

OFFICIAL   3ᵈ   PROGRAMME

Arsenal were also associated with the Rs in the next season (1954/55), but for all the wrong reasons. In the first round of the FA Cup, Rangers drew the amateurs Walthamstow Avenue at home, with the result being a 2-2 draw. The replay at the Avenue ground also finished 2-2 and the decider went to a second replay at Highbury. Rangers were outplayed and the part-timers celebrated a 4-0 thrashing of their Third Division opponents.

The side that lined up for Rangers in the 1956/57 season saw some improvement, finishing tenth in the division. Left to right, back row: Andrews, Finney, Rhodes, R. Springett, M. Powell, Silver, Rutter, Lay, Cameron. Front row: Woods, Angell, Dean, Ingham, Quigley, Longbottom, Petchey, Hellawell. Their record was played 46, won 18, drawn 11 and lost 17 with 47 points. The team scored 61 goals and conceded 60.

The 1957/58 season consolidated QPR's League form and the team finished tenth again. It was an important position as it put the Rangers into the new Third Division for the 1958/59 season. The north and south Third Division split was abandoned in favour of a third and fourth division competition. The FA Cup, however, brought more embarrassment as in an away tie at Hereford they were beaten 6-1 by the non-League side. Perhaps the extra training for Temby, Lay, Finney, Woods and Andrews helped improve matters as the results following that game were six draws and one win.

One of the plus points to emerge from this quiet spell in QPR's fortunes was the signing of the elder of the Springett brothers, Ron. Signed from Victoria United in 1953, he became the regular first team 'keeper in 1956 and soon joined the long line of brilliant QPR goalkeepers. He transferred to Sheffield Wednesday in March 1958 where he won 33 caps playing for England.

A change of manager came in August 1959 with the appointment of ex-Ranger Alec Stock and he stepped up the fitness drive. Messrs Woods, R. Springett, Rutter, Ingham and Petchey seem to be getting along quite well with their skipping, but Archie Andrews seems less enthusiastic!

The White City stadium was once again under consideration as the home for the Rangers. Secretary John Smith enquired if any of the member clubs of the Football League were likely to have any objections to a move. In retrospect, he may have wished that there had been some rejections to the proposal.

Bert Baker, Albert Hittinger and George Wodehouse, three men who were each chairman of QPR between 1944 and 1965, meet at the White City to discuss the proposed move to the new stadium. As before the concept looks right, but it would still take good team performances to build the attendance figures.

QUEEN'S PARK
RANGERS

POSTPONED
Waterlogged Pitch

Football League Division III

Monday October 1st 1962

HULL CITY

At White City   Kick off 7.30 p.m.

OFFICIAL   PROGRAMME

6d

Having tried and rejected the idea in 1918 and 1931, Rangers finally decided that once again their future lay at the White City in 1962. All the dignitaries of the FA and the Football League were there for the first match on Monday 1 October 1962. Alas all in vain, the heavens opened up, the rain came down and the match was called off. As far as the White City was concerned, so were QPR at the end of that season – back off to Loftus Road.

Ray Drinkwater joined Rangers from Portsmouth and was the goalkeeper between the Springetts. He was the first choice 'keeper between 1958 and 1963, made 214 appearances and was highly rated by his teamates.

November 1963 saw a sudden disruption to the continuity of the Rangers boardroom. At a shareholders meeting John Bloom (pictured), the Rolls washing machine millionaire, led a potential takeover bid for the club and successfully challenged the adoption of the annual accounts. Writs for slander were served and tempers ran high. In the end the club's board survived but it indicated that the time for new blood in the boardroom was nigh.

One of the players that Alec Stock brought to the club was Brian Bedford, a twenty-six-year-old centre forward from Bournemouth. During his six year spell from 1959 to 1965 he scored 180 goals in 283 appearances, coming close to George Goddard's club record. This picture shows a typical Bedford goal, outjumping the Port Vale defenders to score in the 3-0 win in April 1964.

Jimmy Andrews came to Rangers around the same time that Alec Stock became manager. After two years he retired from playing and became a much-respected team coach.

Alec Stock's shrewd buying and the development of a number of the club's younger players indicated that better times were coming – albeit slowly. The squad for the 1964/65 campaign was, from left to right, back row: Sibley, Keen, Taylor, Gibbs. Middle row: Andrews (coach), McLeod, R. Brady, Smith, P. Springett, Vafiadis, McQuade, Farmer (trainer). Front row: Collins, P. Brady, Angell, Bedford, Nelson. QPR finished the season in fourteenth with a record of played 46, won 17, drawn 12 and lost 17 with 46 points. They netted 72 times but conceded 80 goals.

The changes in the boardroom finally arrived on 12 March 1965 when Jim Gregory assumed the chairmanship of the club and a new era dawned. He met with the directors that would work alongside him to plan the future of Queens Park Rangers.

Four

Gregory and the Glory Days
1965-1979

1965/66: Gregory and Stock start the team rebuilding by signing Lazarus, Sanderson, Langley and Marsh. The young players are blooded.

1966/67: QPR become the first ever Third Division club to win a major final at Wembley. The League Cup win goes alongside the Third Division championship.

1967/68: Runners-up in Division Two and into the top flight. Docherty manages for twenty-eight days and then departs. Les Allen appointed.

1968/69: Out of their depth – relegated with only 18 points. Gregory starts rebuilding the stadium. South Africa Road stand opened.

1969/70: Back in Division Two. Venables signs. Finish ninth.

1970/71: Gordon Jago takes over in January. Parkes proves an excellent signing.

1971/72: Rodney Marsh becomes Rangers' second English international. Later in the season he was sold to Manchester City. The rebuilt Ellerslie Road stand is opened.

1972/73: Promotion again to the top division. Clement, Francis, Gillard, Hazell and Leach mature. Thomas, Givens and Bowles are signed. Givens capped for Republic of Ireland.

1973/74: Finish eighth in Division One. Parkes and Bowles capped for England, McLintock signed from Arsenal. Crowds hit record levels of over 30,000.

1974/75: Dave Sexton appointed manager. Francis, Gillard and Thomas play for England. Masson and Webb signed. Team finish eleventh in Divisison One.

1975/76: QPR finish as runners-up to Liverpool in Division One.

1976/77: Reach semi-finals of League Cup and quarter-finals of UEFA Cup. League form drops and only finish fourteenth in Division One.

1977/78: Frank Sibley appointed manager. Finish nineteenth in Division One. Parkes goes to West Ham for a record £565,000.

1978/79: Steve Burtenshaw in charge for one season. Rangers relegated.

The youth team that won the South-East Counties League championship in 1963/64. A number of these players were to make substantial contributions to the success of QPR in the late sixties and early seventies. Left to right, back row: Hunt, Nash, P. Springett, Jacks, Hazell, Blake. Front row: Vaffiadis, R. Morgan, Leach, Sibley, I. Morgan.

Frank Sibley, an England youth international who played in the 1967 League Cup final, had his playing career curtailed by a major injury in the early seventies. Later, however, he was an important member of Rangers' backroom staff and he remains today a highly respected coach. In July 1977 he had a one year spell as manager of the club and was recalled for a second term as caretaker boss in the early months of 1985.

Pre-season July 1965 and cricket is in fashion – as shown by players Peter Springett, Brian Bedford and Mike Keen (batting).

Signed in 1965, Les Allen brought the experience of winning from his days with Tottenham. He played 153 games over four successful seasons and coupled that with netting 62 goals. His signing for Rangers signalled the first of the family's connections – Clive, Martin and Bradley Allen were to follow.

In 1965/66 Rangers started to show their potential and they finished third in Division Three. In this shot Ron Hunt and Ian Watson challenge Watford's Ron Saunders in the 2-1 win at Vicarage Road in March 1966.

Queens Park Rangers against West Bromwich Albion in 1967 was the first League Cup final to be played at Wembley. The club were the first team to reach a major Wembley final while members of the Third Division. Rangers supporters decided to start their special day early. The fans walk from Loftus Road with the famous QPR drum much in evidence – they danced all the way home!

The match programme and ticket for the greatest day in the club's history. They are collectors' items for any Rangers fan.

An atttendance of 100,000 watched the match and the the mixing of the fans brought about no ill feeling, but instead built-up the atmosphere – the fans' great day out had arrived and they were going to enjoy it! The West Bromwich followers were first to rejoice as their team went 2-0 up in the first half. However, it was Rangers fans who went home happy as the team fought back to win by three goals to two.

Shepherd, the WBA goalkeeper, finishes up on the deck with QPR's Ron Hunt, the ball runs loose and Lazarus crashes in the winner. Seen here, he peels away after netting with Roger

Morgan and Rodney Marsh anxiously looking on. The referee signalled goal and Rangers became the first Division Three team to win a Wembley final.

Les Allen, Jim Gregory and Alec Farmer enjoying the dressing room celebration of the greatest single day in Rangers' history. Alec Farmer, who joined QPR as a player in 1934, seems to be reflecting how the times have changed.

Mike Keen skippered the side in the final. Signed by Rangers in 1959, he was the first of many fine young players developed by Alec Stock and he was a regular first team member throughout the sixties, clocking up some 440 appearances.

In March 1966, Gregory and Stock had made what was possibly the one single decision that ultimately cast the future of the football club. Fulham had overspent on new players as they battled to defend their First Division status and so agreed to sell Rodney Marsh to Rangers for £15,000. Credit should go to Marsh for agreeing to go down two divisions, and his judgement was the making of him and the start of something big at Loftus Road. In this photograph Marsh moves in on Hull 'keeper McKechnie in March 1969.

The 1966/67 season ended and Len Shipman, the president of the Football League, came to Loftus Road to present Jim Gregory with the newly won Third Division championship and also to host the club presentation of the League Cup. Those shown here are Ron Philips the secretary, Len Shipman, Alec Stock and Jim Gregory.

The team that did the double of Division Three championship and League Cup winners in 1966/67. Left to right, back row: R. Morgan, Sibley, Lazarus. Middle row: Watson, Leach, P. Springett, Kelly, Wilks, Langley. Front row: Marsh, I. Morgan, Hazell, Keen (captain), Allen, Hunt, Sanderson. The League record was played 46, won 26, drawn 15 and lost 5 with 67 points. The team netted 103 times and conceded only 38.

The progress that QPR had made in such a short time brought concerns that the club might struggle in the Second Division. Alec Stock and chairman Gregory strengthened the playing staff by welcoming new boy Allan Harris from Chelsea and also the return of Ron Springett to Loftus Road in July 1967.

86

Left: The 1967/68 season saw Rangers continuing their forward march with the help of an own goal from Aston Villa in the last game of the season on 4 May 1968. The 2-1 win gave the club promotion to the top division. It was heady stuff for the Rangers fans but the players seemed to be enjoying it too. Those pictured are, from left to right, back row: Wilks, Leach, Clarke, Keen, Harris, Hazell. Front row: Kelly, Keetch, the mascot, Ian Morgan, Allen. QPR's record for the season was played 42, won 25, drawn 8 and lost 9 with 58 points. They scored 67 goals and conceded 36. *Right*: In the summer of 1968 Les Allen was appointed the manager for QPR's first season in the top flight. Team strengthening commenced with the signing of Terry Venables from Tottenham Hotspur for £70,000. Over the next six seasons he would captain the club and play 206 games in a Rangers shirt.

Phil Parkes, a promising nineteen-year-old goalkeeper, also joined Rangers from Walsall in June 1970. He fulfilled all of those expectations, playing over 400 games for the club as well as being capped by England. The sale of Parkes to West Ham in 1979 for £565,000 was much in line with chairman Jim Gregory's general philosophy that at a club such as Rangers, you always had to sell if the offer was above what he and the manager thought the player was worth, given the player's age and what you could get if you invested in a quality replacement. In July 1979 the club signed nineteen-year-old Chris Woods for £250,000 and in due course he also went on to play for England.

The growing stature of Queens Park Rangers was endorsed when Messrs Clements, Parkes, Venables, Francis and Marsh won the London Five-a-Side competition in May 1971.

Rodney Marsh, QPR's first English international for sixty-three years, was in demand and the club eventually sold the fans' idol to Manchester City in March 1972 for £ 200,000. He had played 242 games in the hooped shirt and had a tremendous goal scoring record of 134 goals. His ability and extrovert character had been a major force in Rangers' rise to the top echelons of the Football League. Without question he is one of the truly great players of the club.

Left: Gordon Jago, Les Allen's assistant, takes command in 1973 and at this stage does not seem to have convinced his chairman! *Right*: The king has gone, welcome the new king. Stanley Bowles was seen as a high-risk signing in 1972, but proved to be inspirational. While often in the news, he managed to leave any controversy in the dressing room and performed brilliantly in a talented QPR team. He occasionally went missing from training sessions and was late arriving for matches but out on the pitch his talent was awesome.

Gordon Jago stated during the 1972/73 pre-season that he believed he had a team that would get promotion to the top division and so it proved, with Rangers finishing as runners-up to Burnley. These were the players that were in at the start of some great years for QPR. Left to right, back row: Hazell, Ferguson, Clement, Parkes, Evans, Gillard. Front row: Bowles, Francis, Busby, Venables (captain), Givens, Leach. The team's record for this season was played 42, won 24, drawn 13 and lost 5 with 61 points, 81 goals for and 37 against.

Pre-season training is underway and team spirit seems to be good as manager Gordon Jago lends support to Messrs Venables, Givens and Bowles.

The year 1973 was a great one for Terry Mancini, who is seen here under pressure from Mike Pejic of Stoke City. He joined Rangers from Leyton Orient aged twenty-nine and in his first season won a Second Division runners-up medal. The following season he played First Division football for the first time in his career and gained international recognition for the Republic of Ireland.

Dave Sexton was sacked by Chelsea in October 1974 and joined QPR as manager one week later. He took the club to the First Division runners-up slot in 1975/76, Rangers' highest ever League position. His low profile hid a tremendous tactical awareness, which ultimately led Manchester United to draw him to bigger challenges at Old Trafford.

Proud and happy to represent their country: Dave Thomas gained 8 caps and Gerry Francis gained 12. Their international selection shows the progress the club had made over the previous ten years. Gerry also received the honour of being appointed England captain.

While some Rangers stars were breaking into the England team, Don Givens was playing regularly for the Republic of Ireland. He made some 56 appearances for his country, scoring 19 goals. He also picked up rave notices resulting from his goalscoring for QPR. In the season that they finished runners-up to Liverpool he missed only one game and was the leading goalscorer with 13 goals.

Frank McLintock was thirty-three when he joined Rangers from Arsenal, where he had a distinguished career. He was voted Footballer of the Year and was a winner of the double while at Highbury. McLintock was an inspired signing who brought experience and reliability to Rangers' defensive play from the 1973/74 season to 1976/77.

Alongside McLintock was Dave Webb, that great competitor who gave QPR over three years of uncontainable enthusiasm and commitment. Webb joined Rangers in July 1974 at the age of twenty-eight and made 147 appearances for the club – all in the top division. He added to a distinguished career at Southampton and Chelsea.

Micky Leach gratuated from the junior ranks and was greatly respected by his colleagues as a team player. He played for the Rs for fourteen years and made 361 appearances before departing to the USA to play for the Detroit Express in March 1978.

Dave Sexton's 1975/76 side had a good balance between constructive football and aggressive play. The Division One championship was only lost on the last day of the season when Liverpool won at Wolverhampton. The squad was, from left to right, back row: Rogers, Beck, Givens, Cunningham, Pritchett, Westwood, Thomas. Middle row: Bowles, Shanks, Busby, Teale, Parkes, Abbott, Leach, Gillard. Front row: Webb, McLintock, Clement, Francis, Hollins, Masson. Their record was played 42, won 24, drawn 11 and lost 7 with 59 points, 67 goals for and 33 against.

As Division One runners-up, Rangers qualified for the UEFA Cup in 1976/77. Preparation was intense for the tie against Cologne in November 1976. Webb, Masson and Thomas show enthusiasm in training for the match ahead.

While others trained, Dave Clements fought to get fit. He made it and Rangers went on to a resounding 3-0 home win. Although they lost the return leg in Germany 1-4, they went through on away goals.

In the quarter-final of the UEFA Cup in March 1977 the club were drawn at home to AEK Athens and got a great start, winning the first leg at Loftus Road 3-0. Here, Gerry Francis nets the first of his two penalty goals in that game while Givens and Thomas look on. The return leg resulted in a 3-0 defeat and the game went to a penalty shoot-out where Rangers were eliminated on penalties by seven goals to six.

John Hollis gives a great ball to Dave Thomas and seems happy to leave it to him to sort out the Stoke City defenders in March 1977.

February 1978 saw Rangers drawn at home to Nottingham Forest, a game which finished 1-1. Here, Rangers line up to defend a Forest free-kick. The Rangers players are, from left to right: Gillard, Busby, James, Shanks, Bowles, Givens. However, there seem to be more legs than players!

Five

Synthetic and Successful

1979-1988

1979/80: Tommy Docherty returns in May 1979 and signs Tony Currie, Bob Hazell and Steve Wicks. Nineteen-year-old Clive Allen is sold to Arsenal for £1 million.

1980/81: School End Terrace and Stand completed. Terry Venables joins from Crystal Palace as the new manager. Many new signings include Stainrod and Fenwick.

1981/82: Rangers install the first artificial playing surface amid controversy. Finish fifth in the Second Division and reach their first ever FA Cup final, unluckily losing to Tottenham Hotspur 1-0 after a replay. Reserves win the Combination and the youth team win the South East Counties League.

1982/83: Finish top of Division Two and gain promotion. Les Ferdinand and John Gregory come in to strengthen the squad. The Division One clubs complain about the Omniturf pitch and try to get it banned.

1983/84: Loftus Road Stand finished and the major ground rebuilding now completed. Rangers finish fifth in the top flight.

1984/85: Venables leaves for Barcelona, Alan Mullery takes over for six months. Jim Smith appointed in July 1985. Reach second round of the UEFA Cup.

1985/86: World Championship boxing at Rangers Stadium. QPR thirteenth in Division One and reach the final of the League Cup, losing to Oxford United 3-0.

1986/87: David Seaman signed from Birmingham. The club finish sixteenth in the League. In May 1987 Jim Gregory retires as chairman. David Bulstrode becomes the new owner with controversial plans for merging with Fulham.

1987/88: The club finishes fifth and at the season's end Bulstrode returns the club to playing on a natural grass surface.

1988/89: Bulstrode dies suddenly and Richard Thompson takes control of the club.

Tommy Docherty came for his second spell as manager in May 1979 and in August he signed England international Tony Currie from Leeds for £400,000. A great talent and a player capable of controlling a game from midfield, he spent four years with the club, playing around 100 matches.

After hectic trading in 1979/80, manager Docherty finally has his team together. Left to right, back row: Gillard, Hucker, Howe, Pape, Wicks, Woods, Busby. Middle row: Kerslake, Currie, Rogers, Stewart, Hazell, Micklewhite, Shanks, Walsh. Front row: Shellito (trainer), Burke, McCreery, Roeder, Goddard, Neal, Waddock, Wilkins, Docherty (manager). QPR finished fifth during this season with a record of played 42, won 18, drawn 13 and lost 11 with 49 points. The team netted 75 times and conceded 53 times.

Tommy Docherty had a great belief in identifying and developing new young talent and he quickly recognised the ability of seventeen-year-old Gary Waddock. He signed professional forms in 1979 and quickly became a first team regular. Very competitive and very busy in the Rangers midfield, he became the darling of the fans. Waddock gained more than 20 caps for the Republic of Ireland and played some 240 games for the Rs. A severe injury had apparently ended his career in 1987, but he went off to play for Charleroi in Belgium and subsequently played League football in England for Millwall, Bristol Rovers and Luton Town.

Early in the 1980/81 season Terry Venables took over the manager's role, appointing Alan Harris as his coach. This was a combination that worked well for Rangers over the next four years. Having joining QPR from Crystal Palace, Venables then went back to his former club to sign John Burridge, Mike Flanagan, Terry Fenwick and later Tony Sealy.

The close season of 1981 saw the installation of executive boxes and the laying of the Omniturf synthetic pitch, and with it came many new marketing opportunities for the stadium. Before the match the sponsors used the artificial surface to promote their company and its products, along with the entertainment of their customers.

"I don't mind cleaning the dressing rooms, but to Hoover the ruddy pitch every Friday..."

DAILY MAIL — SEPTEMBER 4, 1981.

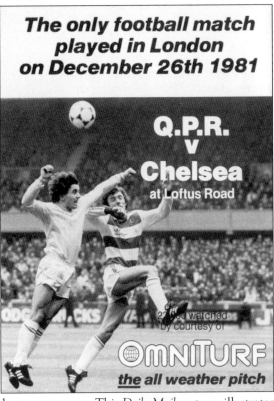

Left: The Omniturf surface caused tremendous controversy. This *Daily Mail* cartoon illustrates the lighter side of the debate. Meanwhile, members of the Football League tried but failed to get artificial surfaces banned because the FA's rules did not specify what surfaces were allowable – a team could have played on concrete! Other clubs who saw the commercial opprtunities quickly followed, including Luton, Preston and Oldham. *Right*: Boxing Day 1981 and Omniturf make their point, advertising the 'all weather surface'. It was not so good for Rangers as they lost 2-0 to neighbours Chelsea.

100

After beating Crystal Palace in the sixth round of the FA Cup, the chance of journeying to the twin towers of Wembley was becoming a distinct possibility. This became a reality after the 1-0 semi-final win at Highbury. Clive Allen was the scorer of the crucial winning goal and is seen here turning inside the West Brom defenders while Simon Stainrod (partly visible on extreme left) waits for a possible loose ball.

The fans of the less glamorous clubs respond to sudden glory and success in a way that is characteristic of clubs like QPR. The FA Cup final was a Queens Park Rangers high that may never be bettered and these fans show how all Rangers supporters felt.

The FA Cup final presentations. Princess Anne is accompanied by Bert Millachip of the FA and they are being introduced by Glenn Roeder to the Rangers team, from left to right: Peter Hucker, Simon Stainrod, John Gregory (shaking hands), Mike Flanagan, Terry Fenwick, Gary Waddock, Clive Allen.

Queens Park Rangers against Tottenham Hotspur in the 1982 FA Cup final. This event stands alongside the Football League Cup win in 1967 and the Division One runners-up position in 1975/76 as the Rangers greatest achievements. This late Terry Fenwick goal earned a 1-1 draw in the final at Wembley, resulting in a replay on the following Thursday.

Bob Hazell, signed from Wolves in September 1979, had four good years with the club. Here, he tackles Garth Crooks during the 1982 FA Cup final. The following season he was anchor man in the QPR side that won the Division Two championship.

Left: In 1981 Tony Currie stated that he would never go to a Wembley Cup final unless he went as a player. A year later on 22 May 1982 he fulfilled that dream. Early action brought a committed tackle from Paul Miller, who prevents Currie getting a clear shot on the Spurs goal. Spurs' Micky Hazard looks on. *Right*: The final went to a replay but Rangers, the better team on the night, lost to an early penalty converted by Glenn Hoddle.

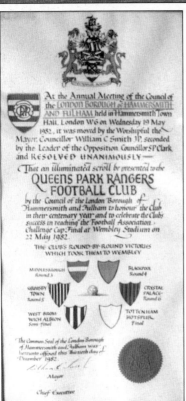

At the Annual Meeting of the Council of
the LONDON BOROUGH OF HAMMERSMITH
AND FULHAM held in Hammersmith Town
Hall, London W6 on Wednesday 19 May
1982, it was moved by the Worshipful the
Mayor, Councillor William C Smith JP, seconded
by the Leader of the Opposition Councillor S P Clark
and RESOLVED UNANIMOUSLY—

That an illuminated scroll be presented to the

QUEENS PARK RANGERS
FOOTBALL CLUB

by the Council of the London Borough of
Hammersmith and Fulham to honour the Club
in their centenary year and to celebrate the Club's
success in reaching the Football Association
Challenge Cup Final at Wembley Stadium on
22 May 1982.

THE CLUB'S ROUND-BY-ROUND VICTORIES
WHICH TOOK THEM TO WEMBLEY

MIDDLESBROUGH   BLACKPOOL
Round 3   Round 4

GRIMSBY   CRYSTAL
TOWN   PALACE
Round 5   Round 6

WEST BROM   TOTTENHAM
WICH ALBION   HOTSPUR
Semi-final   Final

The Common Seal of the London Borough
of Hammersmith and Fulham was
hereunto affixed this Thirtieth day of
December 1982.

Mayor

Chief Executive

The 1981/82 club photograph depicts one of the great
Rangers playing squads. Left to right, back row: Dawes,
Fenwick, Gillard, Howe, Hucker, Wicks, Hazell,
Flanagan, Currie. Front row: Micklewhite, Neill,
Waddock, Roeder (captain), Allen, Gregory, Stainrod.
The team's Division Two record was played 42, won
21, drawn 6 and lost 15 with 69 points, 65 goals for and
43 against. Although QPR had finished fifth in the
League and were FA Cup finalists, more was to come.

The Hammersmith and Fulham Council presented a
scroll to the club which shows Rangers progress
through the cup competition and honours their
achievement. Today it hangs in the club's trophy room.

Same season and Rangers are on the move at all levels. Terry Venables hosts an on-field presentation to Chris Geiler, the youth development officer, and to George Graham, youth team coach, for the success in winning the South East Counties League championship. Theo Foley, the reserve team coach, receives a championship plate for winning the Football Combination.

John Gregory, an outstanding player in Rangers' early '80s success, gained well-deserved caps for England. Here, against Denmark in September 1983, Lauridsen goes in to tackle but Gregory strides on. He played 190 games for Rangers, scoring 43 goals from the midfield.

The end of the 1982/83 season and Rangers are back in the top flight after becoming Division Two champions. Terry Fenwick leads the lap of honour to the delight of the fans. From left to right: Steve Wicks, Tony Sealey, Gary Waddock, Terry Fenwick, Peter Hucker, Gary Micklewhite, Warren Neill, Simon Stainrod. The team's record was played 42, won 26, drawn 7 and lost 9 with 85 points. They scored 77 goals and conceded 36.

The years of Jim Gregory's leadership had brought success to the club but in addition he also redeveloped the stadium from a tip in 1964 to a fine stadium for watching in comfort, while still remaining close to the action. The ground became an arena that the players and the fans still enjoy today.

QPR against Newcastle United on 22 September 1984 was one of the great games at the Rangers' stadium. Rangers were 0-4 down – and out – at half time. Then it all changed with QPR fighting back to get to 3-4. Newcastle got a fifth and time was running out. Wicks scored a Rangers fourth, but the dying minutes edged away and with ninety minutes on the clock it seemed over, but up popped Gary Micklewhite to seal a great 5-5 draw. This picture shows one of the many incidents in a memorable game: Glenn Roeder, Rangers' former captain, tries to stop Simon Stainrod closing in on goal. Anderson covers for Newcastle while Beardsley looks on.

Terry Venables departed for Barcelona and Alan Mullery assumed the manager's role in June 1984. His squad was, from left to right, back row: Neill, Waddock, Fillery, McDonald, Fereday, Stewart, Micklewhite. Middle row: Butler (physiotherapist), Charles, Wicks, Hucker, Chivers, Stainrod, Armstrong (reserve team coach). Front row: Mullery (manager), Gregory, Allen, Fenwick, Dawes, Sibley (assistant manager). The record for the 1984/85 season, in which the team finished nineteenth in Division One, was played 42, won 13, drawn 11 and lost 18 with 50 points. They scored 53 goals and conceded 72.

There were a number of events promoted at the stadium after the installation of the artificial surface. Perhaps the highlight of these was the WBA Featherweight Championship of the World fight between McGuigan and Pedroza. A transformed stadium and a great occasion.

Manager Jim Smith alongside Michael Robinson after a hard-earned draw in the Milk Cup semi-final at Liverpool on 5 March 1986. The 2-2 draw saw Rangers through to the final at Wembley by three goals to two after they had won the first leg 1-0 at Loftus Road.

The Milk Cup final on 20 April 1986 saw QPR face Oxford United. Jim Smith leads out Rangers at Wembley with captain Terry Fenwick following. Although they were hot favourites, on the day Rangers never hit any form and were well beaten 3-0 by a side that had been put together by manager Jim Smith prior to joining Rangers.

The end of season presentations and Daphne Biggs, a lifetime worker and fan in the Supporters Club, presents the awards for the 1986/87 season. Robbie James, Alan McDonald and David Seaman are this year's choices by the fans. Rangers finished sixteenth in Division One.

Late in the 1986/87 season, Jim Gregory announces that he will be selling his interest in the club after twenty-two years and he shows his appreciation to club directors Tony Ingham, Tony Williamson, Tony Chandler and Brian Henson at a farewell party.

Right: Jim Gregory joined Queens Park Rangers in March 1964 and over his twenty-two-year tenure he had numerous team managers – eleven in all (and some twice). While not all would appreciate his style of management, they would provide testament to his ability to recognise real talent and the fact that he always encouraged the signing of players who were attractive to watch. *Below left*: The public company Marlar Estates agreed the purchase of QPR and, under the leadership of David Bulstrode, announced that they planned to merge the club with Fulham. The new side would play at Loftus Road under the name of Fulham Park Rangers. The fans of both clubs staged numerous volatile demonstrations against the proposal and it was eventually dropped, with Bulstrode becoming the chairman of QPR. *Below right*: Bulstrode came to Rangers with determination to continue the club's progress and through his association with Fulham he persuaded Paul Parker to join QPR for a bargain fee of £200,000. Paul went on to gain 16 caps for England before his transfer to Manchester United in August 1991 for £2 million. He was also Player of the Year on some three occasions.

Fulham merger creates history in £6m deal

By Christopher Davies

111

While there had been a number of commercial successes with the synthetic surface, it was highly unpopular with both Rangers fans and all the League clubs. In a hectic 1988 close season David Bulstrode prepared for the return to grass. Two weeks after this picture was taken the team were back playing on natural grass and everyone was happy.

Just as the 1988/89 season was getting underway the club was shocked by the sudden death of David Bulstrode. David Thompson took over as the new chairman.

Six
Football Restructures and so do QPR
1989-1999

1989/90: Trevor Francis sacked as manager and Don Howe takes over. Rangers sign Ray Wilkins and spend £1 million on Roy Wegerle. Finish eleventh in First Division.

1990/91: Seaman moves to Arsenal in the close season for £1.3 million and the Czech international Stejskal is signed as replacement.

1991/92: After two seasons Howe is replaced as manager by Gerry Francis. Rangers have their first and only victory over Manchester United at Old Trafford, winning 4-1.

1992/93: The elite Premier League is launched and QPR finish as the top London club in a very creditable fifth. Gates improve to an average of over 14,500.

1993/94: Francis moves on to manage Tottenham and Thompson appoints Ray Wilkins to take charge. Sinton and Peacock are sold, netting over £5 million. The fans become disturbed by a number of player sales and turn against the chairman, who stands down in the close season while retaining financial control.

1994/95: Peter Ellis becomes club chairman. Under-21 international Kevin Gallen makes his first team debut. Rangers finish in eighth position. Les Ferdinand leaves QPR and signs for Newcastle in a £6 million deal, a club record.

1995/96: QPR relegated from the Premier League with only 9 wins out of 38. Chris Wright, the chairman and driving force of Chrysalis, buys out Richard Thompson's interest in the club for a reported £11 million. Hateley is bought for a club record £1.5 million.

1996/97: Ray Wilkins resigns by early September. Chris Wright acquires Wasps RFC and relocates them at Loftus Road. He restructures the two clubs under the Loftus Road PLC banner and floats it on the stockmarket, raising £12 million from the placing. Stewart Houston is appointed manager.

1997/98: In December Houston is sacked after a string of poor results and Ray Harford replaces him. Things get worse and QPR avoid relegation by one point. Their League position is the lowest for thirty-two years. Mike Sheron is signed for £2.35 million.

1998/99: Harford leaves and former player and manager Gerry Francis returns to steady the ship. Following a rights issue the club raise a further £2.3 million from shareholders. The 6-0 defeat of Crystal Palace on the last day of the season keeps the club in Division One.

Trevor Francis looks somewhat amazed. He scored all three in the 3-1 away win at Aston Villa on 23 September 1989 and then got substituted – and he was the manager!

Alan McDonald is Rangers' most capped international player with 52 appearances for Northern Ireland. Joining QPR from the junior ranks in 1981, he made his first team debut in 1983 and went on to play 483 games for the club. He competed for every ball in every game and his duels with Mark Hughes of Manchester United are an outstanding memory of a great Rangers player.

In November 1989 chairman
Thompson, responding to player
unrest, dismissed Trevor Francis and
installed coach Don Howe as the
manager. Howe's first major signing
was the talented Ray Wilkins on a free
transfer from Glasgow Rangers and
here they pick up on a PR opportunity
with the match mascots. Quiet but
much respected in the football world,
Wilkins maintained Rangers in the
top division, holding a mid-table
positon in an increasingly money-led
Football League.

Howe also signed American ball-
playing forward Roy Wegerle, who
became a real favourite among fans
bred on the talents of Marsh, Bowles
and Gerry Francis. Here he goes past
Liverpool defender Hysen with
Houghton looking on in their match
on 28 April 1990. His goal against
Leeds United in October 1990 was up
there with the Rodney Marsh vintage
and was voted Goal of the Season.

Dave Seaman was the second Rangers goalkeeper to be selected to play for England, gaining 3 caps while with the club. Signed in August 1986 by Jim Smith, his reputation grew season by season until after 4 seasons and with 175 Rangers games behind him he moved on to Arsenal in July 1990.

Andy Sinton signed from Brentford in March 1989 and was yet another player to get international recognition after joining Rangers. He gained 10 of his 12 caps while at Loftus Road. Early action at Old Trafford in September 1990 shows him striking for goal while Manchester United's Gary Pallister closes in.

After retiring from playing, Gerry Francis went into club management and after an unsuccessful spell at Exeter he moved to take over at Bristol Rovers. Against all the odds in 1990, Rovers won promotion to Division Two at a time when the Bristol side were losing their Eastville ground. In June 1991 he returned to Loftus Road as team manager and the Rangers finished eleventh in the top division in his first year back.

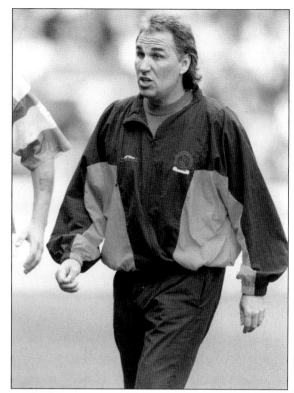

New Years Day in 1992 was a special day for QPR and an extra special one for striker Dennis Bailey. Rangers were playing away to Manchester United in a game screened nationally on television. From the start Rangers took charge and were two goals up at half-time, finally running out winners by four goals to one. Bailey was the hero, scoring a hat-trick. The following day *The Daily Mirror* headlined the sports page 'Massacre'.

Above left: Two quality defenders signed by Don Howe would prove to serve Gerry Francis well. Darren Peacock was bought from Hereford United at a cost of only £350,000 and immediately established himself as a top division player. In 1994 he was sold to Newcastle for £2.7 million after playing over 100 games for Rangers. *Above right*: Clive Wilson, a £450,000 purchase from Chelsea, was another quality signing who, after 110 games for Rangers, quickly followed Gerry Francis to Tottenham after his appointment as their new manager. *Left*: The opening game of the 1994/95 season saw QPR playing Manchester Utd at Old Trafford. Steve Yates wins this duel against Ryan Giggs, but on this occasion the game went to United 2-0. The season ended with Rangers finishing eighth; Tottenham were the only London club to finish higher than QPR.

In November 1994 Gerry
Francis left QPR to manage
Tottenham Hotspur and Ray
Wilkins was made
player/manager. That season he
got the club up to eighth in the
Premiership.

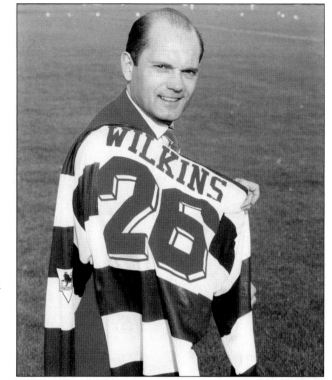

Ray Wilkins watches his side
during the 3-2 defeat of Leeds in
November 1994. Dr Neale
Fraser and Danny Dichio are
the support troops for Les
Bulpin, Frank Sibley, Tony
Roberts and Brian Morris, the
physiotherapist.

In 1993 Rangers' David Bardsley got his first England cap, coming on as a substitute for Arsenal's Lee Dixon. His appearance was limited as he also injured himself and was replaced after only nineteen minutes on the pitch, resulting in one of the shortest international debuts ever. From 1989 to 1997 Bardsley played 294 games for Rangers.

Kevin Gallen came through Rangers youth programme, gaining England Schools, Youth and Under-21 honours on the way. He made a strong impact when promoted to the first team but a bad injury early in the 1996/97 season restricted his progress. Here, he scores against Leeds United in Rangers' 3-2 win in November 1994.

Trevor Sinclair came to Rangers from Blackpool in August 1993 and soon received rave notices, followed quickly by Under-21 caps. Scorer of the Goal of the Season in 1996/97, he moved on to West Ham in January 1998 after 190 appearances for QPR.

Congratulations from Holloway, Sinclair and Maddix go to Les Ferdinand as he celebrates scoring the winning goal in the 2-1 victory over Spurs in May 1995.

In the mid-1990s the structures of various sports were changing with many clubs going for public subscription. Alongside that, Rugby Union clubs were also going professional. Entrepreneur Chris Wright (left) recognised this and bought QPR from Thompson and also took over Wasps Rugby Union club. He brought Wasps to play their home games at Loftus Road and announced his proposal to bring both QPR and Wasps together under a holding company called Loftus Road PLC. In November 1996 he floated the Loftus Road company on the Alternative Investment Market, raising around £6 million for building the two brands.

road plc

(Incorporated and registered in England and Wales under the Companies Act 1985 with Registration No 3197756)

PLACING

of 17,370,000 Ordinary Shares of 50p each of which 2,945,000 Ordinary Shares are subject to recall to satisfy valid applications under the

OFFER FOR SUBSCRIPTION

of up to 2,945,000 Ordinary Shares

by

PEEL, HUNT & COMPANY LIMITED

Nominated adviser and nominated broker to the Company

Karl Ready, another player developed from the junior ranks, has already gained 5 Welsh caps. He is the anchorman in the QPR back line and continues to improve season by season. He has already played over 200 games for the Rangers.

Echoing the changes in the structure of football generally was the growing concern of supporters in the running of their clubs; the fans were looking for a voice. Reflecting this, the 1990s brought about the rise of supporter magazines (fanzines) across all clubs in the Football League. The two most popular at QPR are *A Kick up the Rs* and *In the Loft*.

Alan McDonald leaves QPR after some eighteen years and chairman Chris Wright hosts the club's farewell to a tremendous captain and player for both club and country. All clubs need loyalty and 'Macca' gave 110 per cent along with his substantial contributions to dressing room humour.

Stuart Houston was appointed QPR manager in September 1996 and brought in two experienced Premiership players to lead the anticipated return to the top flight. John Spencer was bought for £2.35 million to provide a regular supply of goals, which he did with 24 in 54 appearances. However, he never settled at Rangers and moved on to Everton in May 1998 for £1.5 million.

The second player, Gavin Peacock, was no stranger to Loftus Road, having come through the club's youth programme in the early 1980s. He returned after spells at Gillingham, Bournemouth, Newcastle and Chelsea and has now established himself as the anchorman in midfield with an ability to get forward and score.

In the penultimate game of the 1997/98 season Rangers got an amazing slice of luck as Pollock of Manchester City heads into his own goal, giving QPR a 2-2 draw. This saved Rangers from relegation and sent Manchester City down to Division Two.

Having failed to make progress with the club, Stewart Houston (left), was replaced by Ray Harford (right) who took over in December 1997. However, his tenure was shorter than Houston's and he was sacked in September 1998 after a string of poor results.

The club turned to Gerry Francis in October 1998 to take the managerial reigns. He had previously left Rangers to manage Spurs in November 1994, but his return was welcomed by the fans looking for someone who had a QPR pedigree. With no money available to improve things he was able to stabilise the club's position in the 1998/99 season.

Danny Maddix was signed at the age of twenty from Spurs in July 1987 on a free transfer. Every season since then he has guaranteed 100 per cent commitment and has gained a reputation as one of the best man markers in the business. With over 300 appearances, he was deservedly voted the supporters Player of the Season in 1998/99. To date he has 2 caps for Jamaica.

Rangers needed to win the final game of the 1998/99 season to stay up. A strange foreboding hung over the occasion but the players turned in an outstanding performance, annihilating Crystal Palace 6-0 to guarantee First Division football at Loftus Road. Here, Chris Kiwomya turns to score Rangers third in a memorable game.

The appointment of Gerry Francis as director of football brought a steadying influence to the club and by achieving Division One survival at the end of 1998/99 he bought time to rebuild the side. With many financial restraints to cope with, he scoured non-League football for players who could perform in the top class. Jermaine Darlington (left), a player who is quick and comfortable on the ball, was signed from Aylesbury United. Stuart Wardley (right) has proved to be an inspired purchase. He was bought at the age of twenty-five from Saffron Walden in the summer of 1999 and Gerry Francis and his coaching staff worked with him through the close season. They converted him from a central defender to an attacking midfield player who is adept at losing his marker and getting forward late to score.

And so to the future. Chairman Chris Wright, alongside directors Nick Blackburn and Peter Ellis, looks out across the stadium prior to the critical game against Crystal Palace in 1999. A 6-0 win ensured that Rangers stayed up and gave enough excitement to compensate for the problems of a difficult season. After that result the next season couldn't come quickly enough for Queens Park Rangers supporters.